MONASTIC WISDOM

Brendan Freeman, OCSO

Come and See

The Monastic Way for Today

MONASTIC WISDOM SERIES

Patrick Hart, ocso, General Editor

Advisory Board

MONASTIC WISDOM SERIES: NUMBER TWENTY-TWO

Come and See

The Monastic Way for Today

by

Brendan Freeman, ocso

Foreword by
Michael Casey, ocso

Cistercian Publications
www.cistercianpublications.org

LITURGICAL PRESS
Collegeville, Minnesota
www.litpress.org

A Cistercian Publications title published by Liturgical Press

Cistercian Publications
Editorial Offices
Abbey of Gethsemani
3642 Monks Road
Trappist, Kentucky 40051
www.cistercianpublications.org

1   2   3   4   5   6   7   8   9

Library of Congress Cataloging-in-Publication Data

Freeman, Brendan.
    Come and see : the monastic way for today / by Brendan Freeman ; foreword by Michael Casey.
        p. cm. — (Monastic wisdom series ; no. 22)
    ISBN 978-0-87907-022-9 — ISBN 978-0-87907-954-3 (e-book)
    1. Monastic and religious life—Congresses. 2. Cistercians—Spiritual life—Congresses. 3. Benedict, Saint, Abbot of Monte Cassino. Regula—Congresses. I. Title. II. Series.

BX2435.F735 2010
255'.12—dc22   2009045359

CONTENTS

FOREWORD

St. Benedict describes the functioning of the abbot's authority in a monastery with three verbs: *docere, constituere, iubere* (RB
2:4). He is to teach, to establish policy, and to give orders. This is
a view of authority that is far more comprehensive than what is
commonly held today. More often than not we think of authority
merely in terms of giving instructions and policing their observance. For St. Benedict, however, the giving of necessary com-
mands is only the visible part of the iceberg. Before arriving at
the point of issuing instructions, the abbot is expected first of all
to create a climate of meaning in the monastery, patiently incul-
cating the beliefs and values according to which monastic life
makes sense. This is his task of teaching. The practical task of
establishing policy follows. The beliefs and values variously
communicated by word and example must be incarnated in structures which bring about a culture that facilitates their observance.
It is within the context of a shared philosophy of life that orders
are given and needful corrections made.

To an outsider a well-ordered monastery seems to function
like a military organization: a defined command structure, con-
formity and uniformity in action, and an insistence on absolute
and immediate obedience. The comparison, however, is decep-
tive. The perfect monastery, if there were one, would be a community that virtually runs itself without the necessity for
multiplying overt interventions of authority. A group of persons
who have internalized the essential beliefs and values and are
safeguarded by suitable structures will not need close or constant
supervision but merely organizational adjustments to suit changing circumstances. Even for less-than-perfect communities

St. Benedict's system works well. He builds into his prescriptions a degree of flexibility which enables accommodation to be made for individual weaknesses, foibles, and particular talents. And there is provision made to bring back into the fold the wandering and even the recalcitrant. Micromanagement was never part of Benedict's plan. In modern terms, the abbot's primary task is leadership; the bulk of managerial functions can be diverted to deans and other officials.

The foundation of this low-intervention approach to the exercise of authority is the abbatial obligation of teaching. An abbot speaking to his monks in the chapter room is not engaging in academic or intellectual discourse. It is to be hoped that there is a sound basis in theology and exegesis but, at this time and in this place, his objective goes beyond the level of the cognitive. His aim is to hold up a mirror before the eyes of his monks so that they may become more fully aware of what they already believe and cherish, and more conscious of the call to incarnate these principles in behavior. The abbot addresses his remarks especially to their hearts and their consciences, reminding them of who they are, who they are called to become, and by what means they can fulfill the purpose for which they left everything to take up life in the monastery.

The abbot's teaching may be considered as ongoing and corporate spiritual formation. If it is well done, when the community comes together to give their counsel on important practical matters (RB 3:1), the options expressed will all fall within the limits of near consensus on the key values by which the community lives. Policy can be established which, although not immutable, endures and is transmitted from one generation of monks to the next. It is within the context of fundamental monastic principles that appointments are made and the management of daily affairs takes place. Likewise, the communal acceptance of the essential components of monastic *conversatio* provides a basis by which errant brethren can be invited to rejoin community practice. This is what St. Benedict terms *correctio*, bringing the wanderer back to the common path, as distinct from *correptio*, rebuking and punishing the deviant to safeguard the common good.

Benedict places a curious limitation on the various levels of abbatial authority: *nihil extra praeceptum Domini* (RB 2:4). The abbot's authority is not his own but is borrowed from Christ. This means that his doctrine cannot be purely his own preferred philosophy of life but must be the fruit of lifelong meditation on Christ's teaching in the Gospel. In the sermons of the Cistercian Fathers of the twelfth century, it is often hard to separate their own words from those of the Scriptures. Such a fusion of horizons was achieved that the Scriptures came alive; no wonder the hearts of their disciples burned.

As can be seen by the example of St. Benedict himself, the content of the abbot's teaching is the transmitted wisdom of monastic tradition. But it is not enough merely to mouth the ancient words; first they need to be internalized and then reexpressed in the context of contemporary monastic experience and the situation of the particular community. This, no doubt, is what Benedict meant when he wrote that the abbot should be sufficiently well trained in the divine law that he has the resources "to bring forth new things and old" (RB 64:9). It is a question not of the dull recycling of tired teaching but of the exposition of a living tradition in a manner that makes that tradition livable.

It is not only by his formal discourses that the abbot teaches: he also instructs and leads by his example. As Benedict says, "let [the abbot] demonstrate good and holy things by deed more than by words" (RB 2:12). I cannot believe that this means the abbot is to limit his verbal teaching to his own performance. If this were done most abbots would scarcely have anything to say at all. It seems to me that what the expression means is that the abbot is to be personally engaged with the content of his preaching; it is more a matter of a goal toward which he strives than a victory already achieved. The abbot draws his conferences from his own struggles with the theological and moral virtues. The insights he communicates are the fruit of personal toil more than the results of study. Curiously, it is by publicly reflecting on his own experience that he attains a greater clarity of moral vision and his own behavior is slowly improved. "When he helps others to amend by his admonitions, his own vices find amendment" (RB 2:40).

Of course, none of this desired improvement in himself or in his community happens very quickly. The abbot might take comfort in the example of the desert elder who instructed his disciple to measure his progress by the rate at which water wears away rock. Instant conversions are rare in a monastery; the most that can be hoped for is a gradual shift in perception. In monastic life, where the laws of cause and effect are suspended, nothing happens very quickly. Patience and perseverance need to be constant companions. On one occasion St. John Chrysostom was asked why he bothered with such elaborate sermons since few people were improved by them; they all went on sinning. His reply was concise: "Yes, they continue to sin, but they sin less boldly."

The office of preaching is always a demanding task and not only because of the soul-searching it provokes. Much more preparation is required than is apparent to the listeners, and sometimes the performance seems to go badly. For example, it is very difficult to find something inspiring to share when one is enduring a more or less prolonged period of spiritual sterility or is wearied by insistent temptation. Speaking to virtually the same group of men in the same place at the same feasts and on the same themes year after year leads many to wonder if they have anything new to offer. This is not because they are confident that anybody remembers what they said last time. Monastic prayer is a low-impact exercise; brilliant flashes of insight are uncommon. Even one who is very faithful to regular prayer will often find himself staring at a blank wall when the time comes to prepare a homily or sermon.

It is in the moments when the feeling of emptiness is most acute that the one called to proclaim the Good News can expect his words to have the greatest power. Preaching is fundamentally a work of faith—on the part of the preacher as well as in the hearts of those who listen. The task is particularly hard in a monastic setting because feedback rarely comes from the community: too often the abbot's remarks seem to be addressed to the uninterested and the somnolent, and instances of passive aggression are not unknown. At times like this he may draw courage from the New Testament admonition, *"Proclaim the word: give yourself to it in season and out of season; correct, rebuke, encourage"* (2 Tim 4:2). He may even learn to shrug off the less-than-enthusiastic reception with the thought that it is his function only to sow the seed or to water it; the growth and fruitfulness come from God.

The communal teaching embodied in abbatial conferences is an essential part of the monastic way of life, and its genre is unique. It is familiar discourse: this is to say the teaching is expressed using insider language, and it concerns issues that are of particular relevance to this particular group. There is no room for pomposity or self-exaltation. There is, however, an insistent need for a keen awareness of individual sensitivities and the avoidance of trenchant criticism or innuendo which, once uttered, may be remembered and resented by the target for a lifetime.

The great Cistercian authors of the twelfth century, especially Bernard, Aelred, and Guerric, are wonderful examples of monastic preachers. Their finest works are the literary versions of the talks they gave to their monks, commenting on the Rule of St. Benedict, marking the various liturgical celebrations, and addressing the practical issues that arise in community life. These discourses are rich in their theological and biblical understanding, yet their most outstanding characteristic is that they are so accessible because they are based on experience. This is not abstract doctrine but a teaching that is concerned with daily life and the practical implementation of the Gospel. Furthermore, without ever losing sight of the moral imperatives that Christian discipleship generates, these eminent preachers strove, above all, to instill in their hearers a strong confidence in the power of Christ's work in the soul.

My first reading of this collection of conferences given to the community of New Melleray by Abbot Brendan Freeman impressed me as being in strong continuity with the long monastic tradition of abbatial teaching. These are friendly reflections on the deep truths of faith and life, drawn from the Scriptures, the liturgy and monastic tradition but inserted very firmly into the particular community to which they are addressed.

Fr Brendan has been a monk of New Melleray for more than fifty years, about half of them as abbot, having been elected for five six-year terms. He has been a source of great stability for the community after a long period of change and is held in great affection by his monks. He brings to his task a wide experience of monastic life and of the Cistercian Order and a refreshing down-to-earth style. His love for his own community and for its particular history shines through on many pages. Moreover, it is clear from these conferences that he has kept up his reading and reflection during this prolonged period of abbatial service.

These pages will give the non-monastic reader a good idea of the way monks think about their life, of some of the issues that they face in community living, and the hope that grounds their confidence and makes possible their perseverance. I am happy that Fr. Brendan has undertaken the labor of making these conferences available to a wider readership and I predict that you, the reader, will find them both enjoyable and helpful.

Fr. Michael Casey, ocso
Tarrawarra Abbey
Victoria, Australia

INTRODUCTION

When Jesus turned around and noticed the two disciples of John following Him, He asked them, "What are you looking for?" They said to Him, "Rabbi (which means Teacher), where do you live?" "Come and see," he answered, so they went to see where he lived, and stayed with him that day. It was about the tenth hour (4 P.M.). (John 1:37-39)

"They stayed with him that day," and for the rest of their lives. Like the disciples, we too have been touched by Jesus. When someone enters the monastery, he is asked the same question Jesus asked the two disciples, "What are you looking for?" Our answer is the same as theirs, we want to see where you live and stay with you.

Jesus never really had a place to live. He was a wandering teacher who had "nowhere to lay his head." Even during his time on earth, he was not identified with a place, a home. He was on the road, moving from village to village, up in the hills, crossing the lake, setting his face toward Jerusalem. He was everywhere. It is the same now. We do not have to go to the Holy Land to see where Jesus lived. He lives everywhere. He lives in us. Our life is a journey with Jesus to the New Jerusalem.

Even though monks take a vow of stability, they are still spiritual pilgrims. The monastery is the place where they stay with Jesus, all day, every day. This book is an invitation to "come and see" how we live in a monastery. The words recorded here were never meant to be published. They were written for a monastic community, with no thought of a wider audience. Perhaps that is good.

Some of the best photographs are taken when people are unaware of being photographed. Once the camera is seen, spontaneity is gone. The primary audience for these talks were the monks of New Melleray Abbey. There was no other audience in mind. Every Sunday the community comes together in the chapter room, and the abbot gives a spiritual conference. Knowing monks as I do, I know these talks have to be brief. There is an old saying that the three most useless things in the world are the moon shining in the day, rain falling on the ocean, and preaching to monks!

Be that as it may, the abbot still has the obligation to preach to his monks. What I have tried to do is to articulate some essential elements of the monastic experience. This is not easy, since we are so close to our own experience. It is hard to stand aside and put into words what you are feeling. This is especially difficult when what you are experiencing is the experience of faith. "Faith is the assurance of things hoped for and the conviction of realities unseen," we read in the letter to the Hebrews (Heb 11:1). If we hope for it, we do not possess it; if we cannot see it, how do we know it? Just that, how do we know it? We know it by faith, and that brings us back to the beginning to start the circle over. The monastic life is, above all, a life lived in faith. It is faith seeking understanding. I can have a firm faith and not be able to articulate it or really understand it. St. Hilary used to say, "I have a firm grasp of something I do not understand." Ideally, we should never speak without having experienced the reality we are talking about. How can you speak of love if you never experienced love in your life; how can you speak of honesty if you have not been honest, or patience if you are impatient? Still we do it all the time, because we are all a mixture of love and hate, honesty and dishonesty, patience and impatience. Even those who walked beside Jesus and stayed with him were a mixture of belief and disbelief—even after his resurrection. We all have a bit of the apostle Thomas in us: "Unless I put my hand into his side, I refuse to believe" (John 20:25). Thank you, blessed Thomas, for saying that, because it elicited from the Risen Lord the consoling words, "Blessed are those who have not seen and yet believe" (John 20:29). That is us. I cannot see what I so ardently believe in, what I stake my whole life on. It is this ardent desire to see and to experience that drives me on. There is great consolation in knowing that we would never desire if we had never experienced something of what we desire. Desire itself is an experience. To desire God is to experience God.

This is why the ancient monks in the desert reacted so strongly against the vice of *acedia*—sloth is the usual English translation of this word, but it seems too weak. Extreme laziness, dullness, or utter boredom might better convey what the early monks meant by *acedia*. *Acedia* is the spiritual illness that cuts desire right out of our heart. From the outside looking in, the life of a monk can look monotonous: doing the same thing day after day, no television, no radio, and no vacation. But from the inside, from the heart of a monk, it is an ardent life, filled with longing and love, filled with desire. If a monk is afflicted with dullness of spirit or *acedia* (sloth), he has no place to go. He loses his focus and wanders helpless in the desert. The monastery is meant to reproduce some elements of the desert, the vast silence, the solitude, the lack of distraction. The great emptiness of the desert mirrors the emptiness of a monk's heart emptied of everything but the desire for God. When the desire for God is gone, what is left? The desert can be a place of emptiness or a place of fullness, depending on how you experience it.

Jesus could have said to the two disciples, "Come and see. I live in the desert." In fact he did say that once: "Come aside into a deserted place and rest awhile with me" (Mark 6:31).

So, here we are in this deserted place experiencing the fullness of life and the emptiness of life, experiencing God's presence and his absence.

I hope these talks give you a better understanding of what keeps a monk going, why he lives the way he lives and what it is he is seeking. After all, we are all on the same path. None of us is on this earth forever; we are all moving toward the end, the end that is a beginning. The secret to a happy journey is the realization that you are not alone. Imprinted in you is the reality you are looking for. Come and see and stay in that place which is your own, the place where the mirror of your soul reflects God the Father, God the Son, and God the Holy Spirit, three relationships that make you who you are. You are on a journey to yourself, the image of God.

In what is called The Last Supper Discourse in John's Gospel, Jesus says to his followers, to us, "I go and prepare a place for you. I will come back again and take you to myself, so that where I am you also may be" (John 14:1). The usual interpretation of these words is that after we die, we will have a place in heaven, for Jesus said, "in my Father's house there are many mansions." But could we not just as well think that even now Jesus wants us to be with him where he is? In his glorified body, Jesus has returned to the Father and has brought our human nature into the inner life of the Blessed Trinity. He wants us there even now, and the way there is through prayer. We have the image of the Trinity within us and prayer opens the door to this place, to the center of our being, where Jesus is always praying and interceding for us to the Father, and the Holy Spirit is there also, coming to our aid and praying for us, crying out, "Abba, Father."

My hope is that these reflections will help you find your true home, your true self. As I mentioned, these talks were written for monks, but the reality is that there is a *monk's desire* in each of us. It is a universal archetype: it is a universal human experience, to long for God. There is a place in our hearts that cannot be shared with anyone, no matter how close and intimate the relationship. This can be experienced as a great emptiness that no human can fill. Thomas Merton calls it a point of nothingness, untouched by sin or illusion. Monks dedicate their whole lives to finding this treasure at the center of their being, because exactly here in this emptiness is where we find God pouring his life into our emptiness so that we are filled with the fullness of God. St. Benedict has one question about those seeking entry into the monastic life, "are they truly seeking God?" If the answer is yes, nothing else need be said. The quest is lifelong, and eventually the emptiness will be filled. Benedict promises that our hearts will expand, and we will run with the unspeakable sweetness of love in the ways of the Lord (RB Prol.). Monastic spirituality appeals to all who are truly seeking God in the depths of their heart.

I begin this book with a presentation of the origins of our Benedictine/Cistercian Order by tracing our roots to our founder, St. Benedict, then some thoughts on Sts. Robert, Alberic, and Stephen, the founders of the Cistercian branch of the Benedictine tree. Since St. Bernard of Clairvaux is *the* theologian of Cistercian spirituality, he too is included in chapter one.

Chapter two covers the special events in the monastic journey. Just as there are special moments that mark important turning points in the life of an individual, such as birthdays, weddings, and anniversaries, so too there are special moments in the life of a monk: the reception of the monastic habit, first profession, solemn profession, and jubilees. The abbot is called upon to address the monk on these special occasions. St. Benedict tells us not to give easy entry to someone who knocks on the monastery door wanting to be a monk. *Test their spirits and see if they are from God*. At New Melleray, we have a six-week observership followed by a month away from the monastery. If the desire to join the monastery persists the observer is invited back to begin another trial period of six months, called a postulancy. Formal steps to full membership, however, only begin with the reception of the novice's habit. After a two-year novitiate, the novice makes first profession of the vows of poverty, chastity, obedience, stability, and conversion of manners. The period of simple vows can last from three to nine years. The Profession of Solemn Vows ends the period of initial formation and marks the beginning of ongoing formation. St. Benedict tells us that he wrote his rule for beginners. The wise monk knows he is just a beginner no matter how long he has been in the monastery. This second chapter contains some homilies preached on the occasion of monks reaching their golden jubilees. Ask them; they will tell you they are just beginners.

Cenobitic or community life is a gift from God and is the heart of Cistercian contemplative life. Living in a community is a gift, a support, and an inspiration to live one's call from the Lord. The monastery is a little church within the larger Church. What goes on here has an influence on the whole body of Christ. None of us operates on a global scale; it is in our family circle, with our friends and the people we work with, that we live out our lives and become who we truly are meant to be. Living in community is difficult. I was going to say it can be difficult but, why leave room for exceptions; it *is* difficult for everyone, without exception. Living with other people is a skill, and it begins by learning to live with oneself. I describe this in chapter three, on the matters of community life.

In chapters four and five, I present some essential values of our monastic life, such as silence and solitude, and the hidden dimension of contemplative life. Living the liturgical life of the Church in the cycles of year, week, and day is the framework of the monastic life. The liturgy is how we experience the life of the Church. The Desert Fathers spoke of three liturgies: the heavenly, the earthly, and the liturgy of the heart, which is the community liturgy continued in the interior cell of the monk's heart. These two chapters comprise the focus of the book, as they highlight the key monastic values for understanding our specific calling and Christian life in general.

We love our Cistercian traditions, but inevitably, we have to face to the challenges of the times, particularly the challenge of expressing our monastic vocation in a modern idiom that responds to the deepest needs of modern people. The ancient monks liked to see themselves as sentinels watching out for the spiritual goods of the populace, comparable to the sentinels stationed on the city walls, warning those inside of any dangers approaching. In our times there is certainly the danger of losing our spirits, our souls. The life of a monk in its incompletion reminds everyone who has eyes to see that we are not in our permanent home; we are just sojourners on earth, looking for our true and everlasting homeland. If you find your soul, your spirit, your heart, your deepest self, you have found the road to heaven in this life. You are home already.

We journey together into the future, like the rest of the ecclesial communities, while living up to our own charism as contemplative cenobites under the direction of the Rule of St. Benedict.

"Come and see" through this book where we as Cistercian monks live, and how we live our calling from the Lord. St. Benedict calls the monastery a "school for the Lord's service" (RB Prol. 45). This school requires not just individuals living side by side but a community where the principles of the Gospel are put into practice every day—a community of brothers (or sisters) whose talents, resources, and energies contribute to help one another in responding with love to the Lord. This book is likewise the fruit of cooperative efforts of many minds and hearts too numerous to mention here. Fr. Tom Yalung, however, must be mentioned by name, as he is the one who typed these chapter talks and homilies and encouraged me to submit them to Cistercian Publications for printing. I extend my sincere thanks to Br. Patrick Hart, ocso, of Gethsemani Abbey, managing editor of the Cistercian Publications Monastic Wisdom Series, for his encouragement and acceptance of these materials for publication and wider distribution. Furthermore, I sincerely thank Fr. Michael Casey, ocso, for honoring this work by his Foreword. My heartfelt thanks go also to the countless sources and inspirations, mentioned and presumed, that have flowed naturally and unnoticed into this book. Thank you too, dear reader, for sharing your time with me as we all strive to listen to the Lord and follow his call—actively in our state of life with a solid contemplative footing.

To paraphrase St. Anselm, we have been created to see God, and we have yet to do what we have been created to do. It is time to wake up from our slumber and begin to do what we are created to do.

Chapter One

TRACING OUR ROOTS

One of the first things a novice learns in the novitiate is the origin of monastic life. The class is not taught at a scholarly level; oftentimes it is not even an organized class. He hears it in refectory readings, chapter talks, and feast day homilies. He learns at the heart level, even though it is basically historical data he is presented. Facts tell only part of the story. It is the bloodline we are after, the connection between the founders of monastic life and the novice's vocation. History has changed dramatically over the almost two thousand years of monastic life. Yet there is a continuity of grace. The impulse that moved St. Anthony to sell all and go into the desert is the same impulse that moves a person to join a Trappist monastery. It is the desire for God alone.

"God alone" is a hallowed phrase in monastic parlance. For centuries, men and women have heard the call of Abraham, to "go forth from the land of your kinsfolk and from your father's house" (Gen 12:1), to live for God alone in a monastery. In this regard, St. Anthony, the Father of Monks; St. Benedict, Father of Western Monasticism; and St. Bernard, the twelfth-century Cistercian, are our contemporaries. They sought what we are seeking. Each one of them has something to tell us about our search. They speak to us through their writings, but more importantly, they speak to us by the way we live; in our monastery, we follow the same basic pattern or style of living they established. Their wisdom is contained in the monastic practices they handed down to us. The practice of silence, the life of prayer, how to live alone with oneself, the proper way to live in community, and the art of loving are all skills that have been handed down from generation to generation through the long history of monastic life.

Cistercian monks from the beginning were lovers of the place and of the brethren. The place means, of course, the locale (if you have ever seen the settings of the seventeen U.S. Cistercian monasteries, you know what beautiful scenic places they are), but it means something more as well; it means the spirit which the place shelters. Monks have been living for 160 years at New Melleray Abbey here in Iowa. The fields planted by the founders are still being planted; the path they walked is still being walked. Their roots are our roots; they are our family.

Here are a few words about the most illustrious members of this family. St. Anthony is called the Father of Monks. He lived in Egypt in the mid-third century and had no intention of starting a worldwide movement. Hearing the Gospel of Matthew being proclaimed in his parish church one Sunday in the Coptic town of Koman in Upper Egypt, he was so moved by the words, "Go, sell what you have and give it to the poor and come follow me" (Matt 19:21), that he did it. He sold what he had and followed Christ into the desert, which is where Jesus begins his public ministry in Mark's Gospel. Anthony is called the first monk, and he used to teach his disciples that the one who sits in solitude and is quiet has won three battles: hearing, speaking, and seeing. Yet against one thing shall he continue to battle—his own heart.

St. Benedict (480–547) was born in Nursia, Italy. He left school as a young man and attempted to live in the hills around Subiaco, much as St. Anthony lived in the wastelands of the Egyptian desert. Like many holy men before him, his reputation grew to such an extent that he came away from his cave and founded a community of men who eventually became the monks of Monte Cassino in central Italy.

Benedict wrote a Rule for Monasteries that has become one of the classics of Western spirituality. To this day, Benedictine and Cistercian monks make their vows "according to the Rule of St. Benedict." His Rule opens with the word *Listen*. This word forms a whole way of living in the world, a contemplative way to live. Monks take a vow of obedience. The Latin word *ob-audire* is a composite and means to listen to. Monks are to listen to God, to their abbot, to their brethren, to the environment in which they live, and above all, to listen to themselves, their true selves. It was said of St. Benedict that he dwelt with himself *habitare secum*. To dwell peacefully with one's self is a skill taught in the monastery. The first lesson is *Listen*.

Sts. Robert, Alberic, and Stephen are the first three abbots of the reformed Abbey of Citeaux. They began their monastic life as Benedictines at Molesme Abbey in Burgundy, France. In 1098, along with eighteen other monks of Molesme, they set out on a new monastic venture. They desired a more radical form of monastic life, one that was more simple and austere, more authentic and silent, than they were experiencing at Molesme. Citeaux, close to Dijon, France, is still the motherhouse of all Cistercian/Trappist monks. The way of life established by these founders is still being lived today all over the world.

At the age of twenty-one, St. Bernard (1090–1153) was the first outsider to join the new community of Citeaux. He came with a company of friends and relatives, and quickly became the shining light of Cistercian life. St. Bernard is truly one of the great charismatic figures of the Middle Ages. A leader, writer, mystic, preacher, and counselor to popes, a saint and doctor of the Church, his legacy is still a source of inspiration and guidance to all who drink from the fountain of his wisdom. His eighty-seven sermons on the Canticle of Canticles are among the Church's great treasures. The marriage bond of Christ and the soul is his theme: ". . . if she [the soul] loves with her whole being, nothing is lacking where everything is given. To love so ardently then is to share the marriage bond; she cannot love so much and not be totally loved, and it is in the perfect union of two hearts that complete and perfect marriage consists."[1]

---

1. *Bernard of Clairvaux: On the Song of Songs*, vol. 4, sermon 83:6 (Kalamazoo, MI: Cistercian Publications, 1980).

The "perfect union of two hearts" is the goal of every marriage and is the goal also of monastic life.

ST. BENEDICT, FATHER OF WESTERN MONASTICISM

Basic Rule: Service in Love Flows from the Eucharist

> ". . . Who is the greater: the one at table or the one who serves? The one at table, surely. Yet here am I among you as one who serves." (Luke 22:27)

It is easy to see how this passage from Luke's Gospel inspired St. Benedict in his Rule. St. Benedict structures his whole Rule around service. He even calls the monastery a school of the Lord's service. But if we look at the context out of which this passage is taken, we see it is Luke's account of the institution of the Eucharist. This leads to the question: what is the connection between the institution narrative and St. Benedict?

Unlike Matthew and Mark, who place Jesus' teaching about service in different places in their Gospels, Luke connects it with the Eucharist. Why? Scholars say he did this to relate it to controversies in the early eucharistic assemblies. Right from the beginning, there were problems. Paul had to correct the Corinthians from overindulging at the eucharistic meal. The Hellenists complained their widows were neglected at the daily distribution of food, and James complained that in the assembly, distinctions were made on the basis of wealth. To show the proper order of things, Luke presents his teaching on service right after the institution narrative at the Last Supper. Jesus is among us as one who serves, not as one who sits at table waiting to be served. It appears to me that Jesus is telling us there is an intimate connection between the Eucharist and humble service to our brothers and sisters, a connection between liturgy and life. The Eucharist teaches us about life, about what is important in life. I do not know of any culture or civilization from time eternal that does not acknowledge the difference between those who serve the table and those who sit at the table. There must be something more than a sociological reversal at work here.

The Eucharist is a mystery and as such cannot be fully understood by reason alone; faith must supplement our reason. But there has to be something we understand about it, something to hold onto and practice. I believe that by washing his disciple's feet, Jesus is telling us something about the mystery of the Eucharist, something easily understood, something as easily understood as, who is more privileged? The one who serves the table? Or the one who sits at the table and is served? What does this tell us about the Eucharist? In the Eucharist, Jesus hands over his body and pours out his blood for us. Jesus' words are repeated every day at the consecration: "This is the cup of my blood . . . it will be shed for you and for all. Do this in memory of me." We know that our blood is our life force, our life. When someone says, "I offer you a cup of my blood," they are saying very graphically that they are offering themselves, their very existence to us. Now, we cannot offer actual blood, but we can serve each other and in this way pour out our blood for the other. St. Benedict calls the monastery a school of the Lord's service. As such, it is a eucharistic school, a place where we connect liturgy and life. However, you do not have to be in a monastery to be in this school. The message is so simple: serve each other and you will fulfill the law of Christ who came among us to serve and not to be served.

St. Benedict was quick to take this key teaching of Jesus and weave it throughout his Rule for monks. He begins chapter 35 on the community meals with the words, "The brothers should serve one another." A few lines later, he repeats it, "serve one another in love." Can you think of a better way to sum up community life? Let the brothers serve one another in love.

St. Benedict reminds us often that in serving one another, we are serving Christ. Although the abbot is warned not to show favoritism in the monastery, St Benedict is careful to point out that there are groupings of monks who need special attention. "Care of the sick," he says, "must rank above and before all else, so that they may truly be served as Christ" (RB 36:1). "Guests are to be received as Christ" (RB 53:1). "Monks are to respect each other out of love for Christ" (cf. RB 72:8).

Benedict has a very clear vision about community life. It is a school where we learn how to live the Gospel teachings. It is a house of God where we learn how to live as Christ lived.

Monastery as the School for the Lord's Service

St. Benedict had several names for the monastery. He called it a "school for the Lord's service," as we saw above. In this school we learn, for example, how to put into practice the teaching of the Gospel where Jesus says, "I am among you as one who serves" (Luke 22:27). Another name is "the House of God." Benedict writes, "No one should be troubled in the house of God." Another one is the "workshop" where the monk toils over the instruments of good works. There are seventy-two of them to keep us occupied.

No matter what name he uses for the monastery, there is one thing for certain: Benedict wanted the monastery to be a place of peace. Monasteries are traditionally constructed in out-of-the-way places, away from the business of the city. Harmony based on right relationships with others, self, and God is the basis of monastic peace. The passage from Ephesians about "supporting each other in love" (Eph 4:2) is one of our ideals of how community life is to be lived. The pace of the monastery is calm and measured. The rhythm of day and night is determined by the liturgical hours of prayer.

Some of the ills of our modern society should not find their way into the monastery. These include things such as stress, pressure, rushing about, and busy-ness. Ambition, power struggles, and control over others have no place here. From this description, one would think that monks glide along on a cloud of peace with no cause for anxiety or concern. Would that it was true. Living in community has its own stress. Jean Vanier, the founder of the L'Arche community in France, knows a lot about living in community. Here are some of his insights that come from experience:

> Community is the place where are revealed all the darkness and anger, jealousies and rivalry hidden in our hearts. Community is a place of pain, because it is a place of loss, a place of conflict and a place of death. But it is also a place of resurrection.[2]

Within the Rule there is another theme that is not antithetical to peace but one we do not usually couple with stillness and recollection. St. Benedict strikes this minor chord right at the beginning of his Rule. In the prologue, the word "run" occurs four times. In one case we are running away so darkness does not overcome us. In the three other cases we are running toward something: the tent of the Lord, good works, and finally, eternal life. A sense of urgency is conveyed. We are not just to be sitting around enjoying contemplative leisure. Of course, the strongest word in the prologue is "battle." The monks are "armed with the strong and noble weapons of obedience to do battle for the true King, Christ the Lord" (RB Prol. 3).

You might conclude from this that monks are in a state of war, and maybe we are. This is not far-fetched. Look around. Our society is in a state of war too. We use the concept all the time. We read about the war against crime, the war against drugs, and the war against terrorism, which is even more real after the attack on 9/11 in New York, the London subway bombings, and the Spanish train system attack. We speak about the war against poverty, and the war against injustice and abuse. We battle abortion and euthanasia. If our society does not battle against all these things, they will overcome us, and we all will become enslaved. But the evils just enumerated—crime, drugs, terrorism, poverty, injustice, and abuse—are really symptoms of a deeper battle. And this is the battle the monks are directed to engage in by the

---

2. Jean Vanier, *From Brokenness to Community* (New York: Paulist Press, 1992), 29.

rule of life set down by St. Benedict. He tells us that his Rule is meant only for those who are willing to give up their own will and embrace obedience. It is the battle of the self. We are taught to eschew such things as selfishness, self-promotion, self-indulgence, self-centeredness, and looking after our own self-interest. Benedict writes explicitly, "No one is to pursue what he judges better for himself, but instead, what he judges better for someone else" (RB 72:7).

This way of living goes against the grain, thus the battle. The model Benedict sets before us is the one we see in the Gospel: mutual service. This is the real field of battle. Our innate instincts are to get our own way at all cost. It is the survival of the fittest. The antidote to this illness is putting the other person's interest before your own.

We have a beautiful synthesis of our life in what Jesus says about himself: "I am among you as one who serves" (Luke 22:27). In our daily Eucharist we are invited to share in the act whereby Jesus pours out his life and hands over his spirit to the Father. The Eucharist makes present the passion, death, and resurrection of Christ. We prove the sincerity of our sharing in this mystery by putting into practice Benedict's injunction: "the brothers are to serve one another" (RB 35:1).

FOUNDERS OF THE CISTERCIAN ORDER (CITEAUX)

The Call to Renunciation and Detachment

We celebrate the feast of our three founders, Sts. Robert, Alberic, and Stephen, but in reality there were twenty-one founders. It is common to mention only the first three abbots of the new foundation. The Rule of St. Benedict gives a lot of power to the abbot, and one of the reasons the twenty-one monks left the Benedictine monastery of Molesme to settle in a place called Citeaux in Burgundy was for a stricter interpretation of the Rule of St. Benedict. But it takes more than an abbot to make a monastery.

Our founders, all twenty-one of them, left one monastery to found another based on certain ideals they had about how the monastic life should be lived. It was not a smooth transition. The first abbot, Robert, was ordered back to his original monastery. No one joined the new group for years. They were on the verge of giving up when St. Bernard arrived and joined with a large group of relatives and friends. After a lot of trouble, they were eventually able to live out their dream.

Now, almost a thousand years later, we are celebrating their memory. It is a good occasion to look at our own calling, our own dream. The Scripture readings chosen for this celebration give us a way of evaluating how we are doing.

The first reading speaks of the call of Abraham (Gen 12:1-4a), a call from God to leave his country and his relationship with his father's house. Each of us is free to interpret what that means for us. The early desert monks thought of Abraham's call as three great renunciations or detachments: "Country" meant all the wealth and riches of the world. "To leave your kindred and relationships" meant the sin and vice that cling to us and become like kindred to us. "To leave our father's house" meant the whole visible world, as opposed to the invisible world of the Spirit.

These are radical renunciations just as are those in the Gospel (Matt 19:27-29), "we have given up everything to follow you," and even more so the ones Paul speaks of: leave your own wisdom and justice, even your own holiness (1 Cor 1:26-31).

What does all this renunciation and detachment mean? It means that each of us is called to go out of ourselves, to go beyond ourselves. It is to take the journey to a new and unknown place. In the letter to the Hebrews, we read that our ancestors set out on the journey not knowing where they were going. They were living on a promise, and they died before the promise was fulfilled.

We too live on a promise. We can demand nothing. Monks have been accused of being Pelagians, making things happen by their own effort. One may think that if we fast or wake at 3:00 A.M., we will become spiritual men. Life is not like that. Life is a

great teacher of detachment. We do not set our program, and
then watch it being fulfilled. We live our life, and then come to
understand it in the light of Scripture. Life is a call to move out
of ourselves. As youth gives way to middle age, we are challenged to detach from perceived ideals. As middle age gives way
to old age, we are forced to give up false ambition and pretenses.
As old age progresses, we are made to detach from physical
health itself, from our body. The world we wanted to create is
slowly taken from us, and something unfamiliar and new re-
places it. It slowly dawns on us that God is calling us and leading
us on, no matter how dark it seems or how unfamiliar the road.
The new self made in the image of Christ is replacing the old self.
We leave ourselves to find ourselves again. Are we good monks?
Are we following our founders? Are we good Christians? Who
are we to judge? Life is teaching us. Let us put ourselves in the
hands of the Lord of Life.

Living a Life of Obedience and Humiliations

As mentioned above, twenty-one monks left the monastery
of Molesme in France in 1098 to go to Citeaux, and with this move
we have the beginning of the Cistercian Order. The first three
abbots, Robert, Alberic, and Stephen, are considered our founders. But the other eighteen, lost to history, live on in us through
their humble lives. They have a lesson to teach us about the hidden life. We ask the question: What does their monastic life teach
us? Then we ask further: What are we willing to learn? How
much are we willing to invest? How open are we to what might
be called the hard sayings in the Rule?

St. Benedict tells us we can judge the seriousness of an as-
pirant by his eagerness for obedience and humiliations. *Opprobria*
is the Latin term for trials or humiliations. For moderns, humiliation is too close to shame. They should not be equated, but still
why would anyone be eager for humiliations?

Our Scripture readings present us with the answer as we
look at the life led by our founders. In the letter to the Hebrews,

they are compared to the patriarchs who lived by faith — setting out on a journey not knowing where they were going. All these "died before receiving any of the things that had been promised" (Heb 11:13). In line with the Gospel, they are identified with those who leave all things to follow Christ (Mark 10:24-30).

Setting out on a journey without a clear goal—dying before you gain anything or leaving all without knowing what you will receive in return—is, at the very least, a risky way to live, if not downright humiliating. Is it not a humiliation for us to live a demanding way of life, giving ourselves to it totally, without seeing the results, without being able to point to something we have acquired, something we have achieved?

To live in the dark this way is an insult to our natural drive to succeed. Our society instills in us a strong competitive sense. We are taught to make things happen by our ingenuity and will-power. To bind our will, to put our ingenuity on temporary hold, is a humiliation. The monastery directs us in another way. The common life dictates that we not stand out, that we blend in with the community, and that we get our sense of worth from God, not from some personal achievement.

We must admit this is a path strewn with humiliations. Leaving all things is not a once-and-for-all decision. It is not even about just material wealth. It also means to leave behind all our defenses, and this opens us to being vulnerable. Pride and vanity die slowly and painfully. Is it not a personal humiliation to let others see our failings, to witness an uncontrollable jealousy or envy at another's success? Is it not an insult to our ego not to be able to contain our anger or our stress or irritability? In the common life of the monastery many things we would like to keep hidden are all too public. It is humiliating!

If we follow the path of the patriarchs, if we leave all and follow Christ, our life will be marked with certain unsteadiness and insecurity. We will be between leaving and finding. We will die without receiving any of the things that had been promised. We will die like Jesus, in the dark. Life "in between" is a humbling experience. The goal is always just ahead; we have a little more

to leave behind, always just a little more. We have our eyes fixed
on the goal in the distance.

For now, we know "that our life is hidden with Christ in
God. But when Christ [our] life is revealed, we too will be revealed with him in glory" (Col 3:3-4).

ST. BERNARD OF CLAIRVAUX, PILLAR OF THE ORDER

Close Relationship between Body and Soul

> As the feast of St. Bernard was approaching, I opened the
> life of St. Bernard, called the *Vita Prima,* at random and my
> eyes fell on the words: "On this matter they (the monks)
> began to be a little suspicious of the sermons in chapter
> addressed to them by their abbot."

Even as far back as the twelfth century, monks were questioning the abbot's chapter talks! I find this encouraging. But why
were Bernard's monks suspicious? They certainly were a fervent
group. I read more about how they lived in great poverty and
then these words: "their bread was produced by the toil of the
brethren from the almost barren earth of that desert place and it
seemed to be made more of grit than of grain and, as with all the
other food they ate, it had almost no flavor."[3] So this is why they
were upset. These men were so fervent that they believed "anything that was a pleasure to eat was a poison to their souls."[4]
They were upset with Abbot Bernard because "he seemed to give
more consideration to the body than to the soul." They were so
upset that they waited for a visit from their bishop, and a dele-
gation of monks brought this complaint to him. The bishop set
them straight by telling them that to refuse the gifts of God, such
as decent food, is to resist the Holy Spirit. End of story.

3. *Vita Prima*, First Life of St. Bernard, trans. Webb and Walker (Maryland:
Newman Press, 1960), 61.
4. Ibid., 60.

There are a lot of things we could say about this story. One in particular speaks to me about Cistercian spirituality. It is this: there is a close connection between body and soul in our monastic life. Architecturally, even the church and the refectory are joined by the cloister. We process from the church to the refectory each day at noon. We listen to a reading just as we do in church. We are nourished in both places.

St. Paul tells us that our bodies are being transformed and molded into a glorified body of Christ (Phil 3:17–4:1). He speaks of our earthly body and our heavenly body. As our earthly body diminishes and grows weak, the spiritual body expands and grows strong. There is a descending movement in our natural body and an ascending movement in our heavenly body. Death is where these two movements meet. Death has been described as the place of our total presence to the world, where our soul has access to our body for the first time, where we share in the glorified body of Christ. Prayer is the element in monastic life that anticipates death. It is referred to in the *Vita Prima*: "The way of life itself helps to establish an inner solitude in the depths of the heart."[5] This inner solitude is the place of prayer, the place where Jesus reveals the Father to us.

Knowing Much of the Love of Christ

Sometimes when speaking to groups in the guesthouse, I am asked the question: "What is the difference between the Benedictines and the Cistercians?" I usually answer that we belong to the same family, but the Cistercians do not have an active apostolate, whereas the Benedictines have schools and seminaries. This usually satisfies them. I do not go into the running battle St. Bernard had with the Cluniac monks or the more recent accusations hurled at the Trappists that they are anti-intellectual. Anti-intellectual is a phrase that is still current in our houses. I am not sure how it started; perhaps it comes from de Rance's

5. Ibid., 60.

reform.[6] But it certainly cannot be used against St. Bernard and our early Fathers.

The virtues enumerated in the book of Sirach (Sir 39:8-14) are applied to St. Bernard as a teacher renowned for learning and wisdom. It is true Cistercians do not focus on academic degrees, the type that can puff up a person, but there is a fullness of learning we all pursue, and Bernard is our guide. *Plenitudo* is a word that comes up frequently in his writings; it means "fullness, abundance, copious."

In the passage from Sirach, we hear the teacher say, "I am filled like the moon at the full, listen to me and bud like a rose growing by a stream of water" (Sir 39:12-13). Bernard is a rose by a stream of water, and he encourages us to read out of the book of our own experience. He tells us what to look for in that book. The rose is our union with Christ, and the stream, the words of Scripture. Bernard is always telling his monks to drink deeply from the water of the Sacred Scriptures. This will nourish the flower of love in their hearts.

Everyone who reads Bernard is astounded at his ability to weave passages of Sacred Scripture into his discourse. His memory was extraordinary. But there is something more vital here that needs recall. The stream of Sacred Scripture flows like an underground river through Bernard's inner life. There is a hidden source of knowledge that Bernard is attentive to, a type of knowledge found only in the school of love. Love itself is a form of knowing. Love was the source of Bernard's reputation as a teacher. It was not his memory or his towering intellect, it was love. Perhaps Origen said it the best: "No one can understand [John's] Gospel unless he has leaned against the breast of Jesus and taken Mary as his Mother."[7] The text from St. John's Gospel used for his feast hints at the source of his great learning. Jesus is speaking to the Father in prayer: "I made known to them your

6. Armand Jean de Rance, 1626–1700, Abbot reformer of La Trappe Monastery in France.

7. As quoted in *RB 80* (Collegeville, MN: Liturgical Press), 360–361.

name, and I will make it known, that the love with which you have loved me may be in them and I in them" (John 17:26).

Bernard speaks out of this fullness of love. One morning Bernard began his chapter talk with the words, "Today the text we are to study is the book of our own experience. You must, therefore, turn your attention inward, each must take note of his own particular awareness."[8]

Contemplating Christ

The word "wisdom" as it appears in the Bible is not easily defined. It has a wide range of meanings. In the Old Testament it can mean professional skill, political sense, discernment, astuteness, knowing how to live in society, and even magic arts. Recently I read a helpful distinction between wisdom and knowledge. The object of wisdom is eternal and unchangeable reality; the object of knowledge is changeable and temporal.

The saints would fall in line with this distinction. The Doctors of the Church are so called not because they were the most intelligent people of their generation. No, it was because they taught the way of the Spirit. They shared the wisdom whose object is unchangeable and eternal. St. Bernard was a doctor in this mode. This is why he is so important to us.

By reading his writings, we can drink in some of his spirit. We do not need to be experts on St. Bernard. What we are looking for is to share in his spirit, in his graces. His writings can make devotion and affection grow in our hearts for him and for the object of his wisdom, the eternal God.

Wisdom and knowledge are both necessary in our life. Bernard once said that zeal without knowledge is unbearable. Where there is violent stirring, discretion is most necessary. For him, this is the ordering of charity. Without it, virtue becomes vice, affections run wild, and there can be no harmony in the Church.

8. *On the Song of Songs,* sermon 3 (Spencer, MA: Cistercian Publications, 1971).

Knowledge and wisdom help us to order all the loves in our life: the love of God and the love of neighbor.

From the perspective of the book of Sirach (Sir 39:8-14), Bernard is seen as a man of wisdom. However, the Gospel (John 17:20-26) tells us he is a man of love. Love is a source of wisdom —*the* source of wisdom.

Contemplation has been defined as "a long look of love." Looking at something or someone is a source of knowledge. Through our eyes we become one with the object; we bring it into our life. When we look with love, the object reveals itself to us in a new way. It discloses its full truth to us. We bring it into our heart.

Bernard had his eyes fixed on one object—the same object as his wisdom—the unchangeable and eternal, but now expressed in the person of Jesus. He is the one who wants the love of the Father to be in us as he is in us.

To contemplate the words of the Gospel is to take the words into our heart, there to become real in us. The words are expressions of a mystery beyond words. Experience what the words say. Experience the love of the Father for Jesus taking place in our heart's deepest core. This is what Bernard teaches.

It is the perfection of our baptism—nothing more, nothing less.

UNDERSTANDING CISTERCIAN TRADITION

The Cistercian Charism

We use the phrase "the Cistercian Charism" or "our Cistercian Charism" often, but what does it mean? Right after the Second Vatican Council, we used the phrase a lot because the council mandated a renewal of religious life when it said: "The appropriate renewal of religious life involves two simultaneous processes: (1) a continuous return to the sources of all Christian life, and to the original inspiration behind a given community, and (2) an adjustment of the community to the changed condition of the times."[9] Implementing the renewal mandated by the council took a lot of our time and energy, and the process of adjustment is still going on. To go back to the original inspiration of our founders, who lived a thousand years ago, is somewhat difficult. It seems much easier to return to the inspiration or charism of more modern founders, such as Catherine McCauley, Nano Nagle, and Mary Frances Clarke. All these women lived around the same period in Dublin, Ireland. At the time, Dublin had one of the worst slums in Europe. Separately these three women went into the slums to help the poor. Two started schools; Catherine Mc-Cauley helped the sick. None of these women set out to found a new congregation. They saw a need and tried to meet it. They were given the grace, the charism to do this. Eventually Catherine McCauley became known as the founder of the Sisters of Mercy; Nano Nagle, of the Sisters of the Presentation of the Blessed Virgin Mary; and Mary Francis Clarke, of the Sisters of Charity of the Blessed Virgin Mary. The sisters in these congregations today can reconstruct the early days of their founders. They know exactly what they were about, in educating the poor or in helping the sick, and so forth.

The founders of Citeaux were in an entirely different situation. They were already monks and there were three founders, or more accurately twenty-one, because twenty-one members left Molesmes to go to Citeaux. Michael Casey affirms it was more of a community event rather than an inspiration coming to a particular individual, like St. Francis of Assisi. The twenty-one monks left Molesmes for one primary reason: they wanted to live the Rule of St. Benedict in a more pure form. A lot of accretions had come into the monastic life from the time of St. Benedict to the time of our founders in 1098. They wanted to return to a more primitive living of the Rule. The word *literal* would not fit their desire. The word they use is *pure*. They introduced some new things into the monastic life, such as the lay brother, a Charter of

Charity, and a General Chapter. None of the things were in the Rule. To describe what they were doing, Michael Casey uses the term *creative fidelity* to express their interpretation of the Rule of St. Benedict.

In 1995, our Abbot General, Dom Bernardo Olivera, wrote a letter on Charismatic Associations, which includes the lay associate programs that many of our monasteries sponsor. He begins by quoting Pope John Paul II in his address to the Synod of Bishops on the religious life: "Extraordinary or simple and humble, charisms are graces of the Holy Spirit which have, directly or indirectly, an ecclesial usefulness, for the edification of the Church, for the good of human persons and for the needs of the world" (*Christifidelis*, no. 24). A charism is a grace of the Holy Spirit for the good of the Body of Christ.

Dom Bernardo then says, "The Cistercian charism has its origin in that monastic tradition of evangelical life found expressed in the Rule of St. Benedict. The Founders of Citeaux gave this tradition a particular form, certain aspects of which were strongly defended by the monasteries of the Strict Observance" (Charismatic Associations). Our Constitutions, above all the first part, the Patrimony, are a good presentation of our charism.

In January 1995, the Abbot General wrote his annual circular letter to the Order, this time on the Constitutions. In this letter he connects the Constitutions to our charism. He says:

> Before everything and first of all, we can say that the Constitutions are the concrete expression of our particular way of following Christ according to the Gospel and the Rule of St. Benedict. Because they have been approved by the Church, they are guaranteed to be an expression of the Gospel message.

He concludes:

> Consequently, our Cistercian charism can be considered as a form of exegesis of the Gospel. It brings out and reveals certain aspects of the Gospel. Because of this, the Constitutions as medium and incarnation of our charism are an in-

strument of evangelical interpretation; they clarify our reading of the Gospel as Cistercian. (Circular Letter 1995)

One clear example of this interpretation is in Matthew 19:12-22, a foundational text for all religious life. It speaks of the parable of the rich young man and Christ's invitation to him to sell all he possessed and follow him. Certain parts of our Constitutions lay out for us how to leave all to follow Christ. The sections on poverty, simplicity, obedience, and silence are all ways for us to leave all. They do not apply to anyone but Cistercians. Our Constitutions are a Cistercian reading of the text of Matthew.

Finally, Dom Bernardo says, "The Constitutions are the lasting expression of our Cistercian charism of the Strict Observance. They express the consciousness that the Order has of itself in this moment in its history. They are, therefore, our letter or our card of ecclesial identification" (ibid).

Dom Bernardo's ideas are truly satisfying. They clearly present the question on the Cistercian charism. When we are asked about what led to the foundation of the Cistercian Order, we can only say that our founders did not want anything new. All they wanted was to return to the observance of the Rule of St. Benedict. In so doing, they created something new. Most authors say the newness was the way they found or refound the balance in the Rule. It lies in the way they emphasized certain aspects of the Rule and the way they took into account the body, mind, and spirit of the individual monks. They extended this insight of balance, harmony, and simplicity even to their buildings. A whole new architecture grew out of the Cistercian reforms. There is evidently no clear one-word answer to what is our charism. It is a multitude of answers.

Values of Cistercian Reform[10]

In 1998, Michael Casey, ocso, gave a conference at Clairvaux in France to a group of lay associates affiliated with the Abbey

---

10. From the chapter talk given on November 7, 2004.

of Citeaux. In it, he mentions five areas that represent the values
of the Cistercian reform that are worth developing and transmit-
ting to the future.

Let me quote Fr. Casey at length to clarify the essence of our
Cistercian charism. He writes:

> The first Cistercians began a manner of living which has
> through the ages attracted, sustained and brought to a happy
> conclusion the lives of tens of thousands of monastic men
> and women. The Cistercian Patrimony is not a matter of life-
> less stones, but a living reality incarnate in the lives and labors
> of innumerable brothers and sisters and expressed explicitly
> by a substantial body of doctrine developed by Cistercian
> authors of all centuries. We inherit from the past not only
> buildings and artifacts, not only a lifestyle that many romanti-
> cally believe has changed little from the Middle Ages, but a
> tradition of life communicated in a thousand humble ways
> from one generation to the next. Beneath the Cistercian reality
> lays a network of beliefs, values and core practices that em-
> body the energy of the charism. The heart of the Cistercian
> Patrimony is a philosophy of life as validly applied to the
> twenty-first century as to the twelfth.[11]

Fr. Michael's five values of the Cistercian reform are: (1)
creative fidelity vis-à-vis the Rule of St. Benedict; (2) austerity,
that is, frugality and simplicity; (3) experience; (4) affectivity, the
school of love; and (5) mysticism. I would like to look at two
values, experience and mysticism.

On experience, Fr. Casey writes that twelfth-century monastic life moved away from the idea that the monk's task was
the performance of certain duties or services to concentrate more
on the quality of his experience. From the consideration of human
beings as created in the divine image and likeness, the Cistercians
developed a spirituality based on the desire for God.

11. Michael Casey, "Toward the Cistercian Millennium," *Tjurunga* 54 (May
1998): 58.

At our solemn profession, three times we sing the phrase, "Receive me, O Lord, according to your word; do not disappoint me in my hope." This says a lot about the expectation we have when we come to the monastery. Everyone hopes for a full life, a rich life, a life where you are really, truly happy and basically satisfied. I know from experience that this can happen in the monastery. It comes from doing something else, not by setting out to be fulfilled, but by setting out to be a monk and living according to some goal beyond ourselves.

Miguel Martinez explains it like this: "At its depths, monasticism constitutes a structural opportunity of being human. The monastic dimension is an anthropological dimension, i.e., universal dimension. Every man and woman carries a monastic dimension within. To profess monastic life within the Order is a way of expressing and channeling the monastic aspect of a human being."[12] We can say, then, that the search for God was understood to coincide with the deepest aspiration of the heart, that is, "human fulfillment and not alienation" (Casey).

This brings us to the second value, mysticism. Fr. Casey writes: "Spiritual experience with a strong affective component is the engine that drove the first Cistercians forward. Mysticism is the unseen concomitant of external lifestyle." He continues: "The mystical teaching of the Cistercians was always biblical; it flowed from an interpretation of scriptural text and strictly maintained itself within their limits. It was not concerned with the extraordinary."[13]

I understand this to mean that as we live in the monastery and follow the common life, practicing the observances, something will happen. We will begin to experience the hidden meaning of what we are doing. We will understand and even taste, in the sense of wisdom, the meaning of this life. No one could persevere

---

12. Quoted by Enrique Mirones Diez, "Nomads or Settlers," *Cistercian Studies Quarterly* 4, no.36 (2001): 516.

13. Michael Casey, "Toward the Cistercian Millennium," *Tjurunga* 54 (May 1998): 58.

to the end without this inner experience. We might not be able to articulate it or explain it but we can recognize it when we hear it in a reading or come across it while reading our Cistercian Fathers. Our life is a beautiful blending of the mystical and the mundane, the human and the divine. They are not in opposition to each other, but one being found in the other.

The monastic life is a structural opportunity to be human, and in seeking God we touch the deepest desire of our heart. This is not a new theory. St. Augustine said that we seek one mystery, God, with another mystery, ourselves, because God's mystery is in us. Our mind cannot be understood even by itself, because it is made in God's image.

St. Bernard had this in mind when he placed self-knowledge as the first thing a young monk has to gain. Self-knowledge has many levels. We seek the mystery of God with or by means of another mystery, ourselves. Coming to the realization that the mystery of God is within us does not confound us but leads us deeper into ourselves, deeper into our true self, deeper into a place where God's life and our life are one, where they are joined, united, and wed. The image of the union of bride and bridegroom was popular with our Cistercian Fathers.

The reading from St. Gregory of Nazianzen at Lauds serves as a fitting conclusion to our reflection. He writes: "What is this new mystery surrounding me? I am both small and great, both lowly and exalted, mortal and immortal, earthly and heavenly. I am to be buried with Christ and to rise again with him, to become a coheir with him, a son of God, and indeed God himself" (Office of Readings, Friday, Thirty-First Week in Ordinary Time).

Elements of Cistercian Formation[14]

Since we have so many guests with us this morning, here for the Vocation Discernment Retreat, I think it is appropriate to explain some basic terms you will hear while you are with us.

14. Chapter talk given on September 5, 2004, at which the participants of the Vocation Discernment Weekend Retreat were present.

The abbot gives what is known as a chapter talk to the community every Sunday. It is an ancient tradition. The word "chapter" has a few different meanings. We speak of the conventual chapter to refer to the gathering of all the solemnly professed members of the community. In this sense, a chapter is a group of people with an entitlement of belonging. In our case, only the solemnly professed have the right to vote on important community decisions, such as the vote to admit someone to solemn vows or to elect an abbot. In New Melleray, we meet every six years for the election of an abbot.

The more common meaning of the word "chapter" refers to the chapters of the Rule of St. Benedict. In previous times, the community would meet every morning in the chapter room and read a small passage of the Rule of St. Benedict, then the abbot would give a commentary on it; hence, the name "chapter talk." In our day, the abbot gives a talk every Sunday on a spiritual topic. It is a more general talk and not restricted to the Rule.

With the presence of our guests for the Vocation Retreat, it is timely for me to share some pointers on the elements of an authentic Cistercian formation. This is the fruit of our meeting at Assumption Abbey in Ava, Missouri, with the abbot's extended council. By way of brainstorming, the group at Ava came up with twelve characteristics of authentic formation. The list does not necessarily refer to the order of importance. Some items are self-evident, but we still noted them.

1. A novice director. This is evident, but for some of our smaller houses, it is not that easy to provide a capable monk to be novice master. At New Melleray, we are blessed with not only a good novice master but with two or three others who could fulfill the role. In other monasteries, at times the abbot had to function also as novice director for a few years until someone else could take over.

2. A group of monks capable of teaching those in formation.

3. Common work. This does not mean working together all the time, but some kind of work in which the newer members

feel they are contributing to the monastery and not just being employed in meaningless work.

4. A good library. This is a good point which we take for granted. It takes years and years to build up a good library. Dom Eamon Fitzgerald, the abbot of Mt. Melleray in Ireland and our Father Immediate, mentioned to me that it was tempting for him to take his three-month sabbatical at New Melleray because of our library. He was impressed with it.

5. A leader for the community, called an abbot. One of the roles of the abbot is to ensure that the community provides the best possible formation it can give. Good leadership is essential. Communities who have a new superior every three or four years have a hard time giving people in formation a sense of stability.

The next five items concern the community itself. We know that after the Holy Spirit, the community is the most important factor in forming new people into monks. So there are several things a community should have to be a formative community.

6. First, the community should be open to receiving new members. This is not as easy as it sounds. To be open means to be a welcoming community. It is a place of hospitality. If you are open to new members, it means you are open to changes. Everyone going through the stages of formation and eventually becoming a solemnly professed monk changes the face of the community. St. Benedict reminds us that there are a variety of characters in any community. We do not restrict admittance to only those who think like us. We have liberals and conservatives, Republicans and Democrats in the community. We have unity within diversity.

7. But there are boundaries, and this brings us to the seventh point: a strong community identity. Every community that opens its doors to new members and welcomes diversity has

to have a strong sense of its own identity. We have to have unity of purpose and a common vision of the monastic life.

8. A healthy community will have good communication between its members. There will be a certain affectivity and warm personal relationships. Problems will be addressed and not just left to fester.

9. A community with healthy relationships fosters growth, both human and spiritual growth.

10. As we would expect, such community is capable of generativity, the passing on of life and the fostering of life. If the community is self-centered, there is no generativity. At one time or another, we may go through a self-centered stage. This is reflected in statements like "I do not get anything out of the liturgy" or "What is in it for me?" Our liturgy is a participation in the prayer of Christ to the Father. The monastic liturgy especially appeals to the Spirit praying within us, not to a lot of externals to catch our attention.

11. A community that is centered on God instead of self is capable of leading a novice into a life of prayer. We are not here for ourselves. We are called together in the name of Jesus. We are a praying community whose practice and example leads the novice deeper into the prayer of his own heart. The monastery is a school where we learn how to pray and serve one another.

12. A community that supports its abbot. An overly critical attitude in a community is a breeding ground for distrust and is divisive.

Because the monastery is a school of love in the Lord's service, formation of a novice or a prospective member is a significant factor in the Cistercian life. Actually, formation is an ongoing aspect of our monastic life.

Modern Economy and Ancient Ideals[15]

During the past week, we had our annual business council meeting to draw up a budget for this coming year. With the increased demands of our casket business and of the farm, there was also a large capital expenditure requirement. Soon we were thinking of additional products, such as raising cattle and selling organic beef. Our lay managers for the casket business and the farm are indeed a great help for us in running our industries. But then it also made me think about our situation ten years from now. Will we be any different from the large European monasteries with their industries run entirely by hired help?

Where do we stand in relationship to the ideal we have of our founders? How do we relate to them in conjunction with our newly proposed infirmary, our planned expansion on the casket plant, and a proposed organic meat business? Will these be mostly staffed and directed by lay people? Is this the direction to go, or do we have to reverse our plans?

In the late 1960s a group of five monks saw how big we were getting; they experienced all the hustle and bustle of 150 young monks. We were busy operating a new alfalfa dehydration plant and adding new wings to an already large monastery. This group desired to go back to the original ideals of poverty and simplicity. They received use of a farm from the bishop of Belleville, Illinois, and started the "ideal" monastic life. They grew wheat and made their own bread. They set their life up with the best intentions in the world. But the experiment only lasted five to six years and then collapsed. I am not sure of the reason for the closure; perhaps it was impossible to re-create the twelfth century. Be that as it may, here we are in the twenty-first century celebrating the feast of our founders and reflecting on our monastic expressions of Cistercian life.

Constance Berman, in her book *The Cistercian Evolution*, claims that most of our early documents were written forty or

15. From the chapter talk of January 26, 2003, the Solemn Feast of the Founders of Cîteaux.

fifty years after the events they describe. For her, they are idealized accounts, not historical accounts. Most scholars do not accept her arguments, but they would all agree that the beginnings and ideals of Citeaux were more complicated than we generally think.

However, the question still remains: how do we stand in relationship to our founders? Are we more like Cluny at Molesme or like Citeaux? One argument could be along the lines that Citeaux always had lay brothers to do the bulk of the work, so the choir monks could chant the Office and study. After all, in our golden age, we had tremendous authors and highly educated men. The case could be made that our hired people are allowing us to have the time necessary to live the Cistercian life. Given our economic situation in modern America, it is impossible to support ourselves and still have everyone attending all the Hours of Prayer. Many monasteries, in fact, do not have Terce and None in choir. This idea of the lay people doing our productive work might be necessary, but it does not appeal to me. I am still struggling with the comparison of the life in the 1960s and the life now. In the 60s we might have had one or two hired hands on the farm or in the alfalfa plant, but in minor roles. We truly supported ourselves by the labor of our hands. We followed the norm given in our present Constitutions which says: "Fidelity to our Cistercian traditions requires that the community's regular income be mainly the fruit of its own work" (no. 41).

This is our ideal, but what do you do when it becomes nearly impossible to fulfill? What if you do not have the monks to do the work? You do the best you can and entrust the rest to God. After all, God is in charge. There is a reason why the evolution of our community and religious life in general is going the way it is. No doubt, there are many superficial answers based on sociological and even theological reasons for lack of vocation to the priesthood and religious life, but ultimately, it is a mystery. A monastic vocation is a mysterious grace given to some and not to others. Monasteries close because of the lack of vocations, and somewhere else in the world new monasteries open and are full of vocations. But if you happen to be in one that is struggling to survive, one where the community has to adapt the ideals of the life to fit the reality of the situation, then you have to look around for some reasons or explanations that help you understand what is happening.

Circumstances require us, if not to give up our ideals of supporting ourselves by manual labor, at least to alter them. We are being called to give up, in a sense, one of our children. After all, our ideals can be as close to us as giving birth to a child. We give birth and nurture our ideals. But we are asked to make a painful separation, a renunciation for a greater good, when we have to make a choice of leaving an ideal aside, or at least not being able to live it as we think we should. The greater good is the surrender to God's will manifested to us by the events of the times we live in. The mystery of God's providence hidden in history, the history of the Church, say, in the last forty years, calls forth our faith and trust.

This situation is an opportunity to grow in renunciation. It is a time of surrender. God made a promise to Abraham that his renunciation would be small compared to his future. Jesus promised that those who leave all to follow him will receive more in return. We live on this promise, struggling to leave all during each season of our life.

Monasteries Helping Each Other

In the Cistercian Order, when a monastery becomes so large that it is difficult to receive new members, a foundation is proposed. New Melleray is a foundation of Mt. Melleray in Ireland. This system is known as the Mother House–Daughter House filiation. The abbot of the Mother House makes an official visitation of the Daughter House every two years. On June 8, 2005, we had a visitation from Dom Eamon Fitzgerald of Mt. Melleray in Ireland.

The abbot of the Mother House in relation to the Daughter House is called the "Father Immediate." We have three daughter houses: Assumption Abbey (Missouri), Mt. St. Bernard (England), and Our Lady of the Mississippi Abbey (Dubuque). Every monastery of nuns has a monks' monastery as their Father Immediate.

Our Father Immediate, Dom Eamon of Mt. Melleray, has seven daughter houses, five of monks and two of nuns. These houses are on four different continents. So Dom Eamon is gone a lot. In 2003, he could not make his visitation to us because he had just returned from Africa. He delegated our visitation to an abbot of our choice.

Several years ago the General Chapter produced a new statute on the regular visitation. It states the purpose of the regular visitation as: "To motivate the brothers to lead the Cistercian life with renewed spiritual vigilance and to strengthen, supplement and when needed, correct the pastoral action of the local abbot" (no. 2).

It also says that a "shared understanding between the Visitor, the Community to be visited, and the superior is crucial for the abiding fruitfulness of the Visitation" (no. 6). The statute has four small paragraphs on preparation for a visitation. The first is prayer to the Holy Spirit asking for divine guidance. The second is for the local superior to give a talk or two on the upcoming visitation and to encourage all to be open and honest. The community should not feel any restraint and should be totally free to say what they want. Then the community examines itself concerning its needs at this moment in history. The text suggests the possibility of a community dialog to identify a few major themes for the visitor to address. Finally, the visitor must inform himself as best he can on everything concerning the community he will visit (no. 15).

Different areas of community life could be brought up during the visitation. Fourteen items are listed, such as the level of charity, the spirit and celebration of the liturgy, the balance between *lectio*, prayer, and work, silence and enclosure, hospitality, relations with the Order and the local Church, and even the physical health of the community. This suggested list of items helps to identify areas that can be brought up in the private interviews with the visitor. Writing a paragraph or two on the state of the community as we see it also helps the visitor to understand us. The visitor may not be able to solve our problems, but it will help him to know what we think, our strong points and weak points, where we are succeeding and where we are failing.

Visitation at Tautra Mariakloster, Norway

I made the visitation as the Father Immediate of our Trappistine foundation on Tautra Island, Norway, on June 1–14, 2004. Tautra, as it is known, was founded from Our Lady of the Mississippi Abbey in Dubuque in 1999.

There are eight sisters in the community. The main issue at this point was to petition the next General Chapter in October 2005 to become a simple priory. True enough, in that chapter the foundation's petition was accepted.

This is the first step in a series that goes like this: from a foundation, the new community becomes a simple priory, then a major priory, and finally, an abbey. The only difference between a simple priory and a major priory is that a simple priory has a right to receive personnel and financial help from the founding house. It is a big step to become a priory. A foundation is still part of the founding house, and so the abbess is still the superior of the foundation. Once a foundation becomes a priory, they are autonomous, and the founding abbess has no more authority over it. She does have the obligation of personnel and financial assistance, however, until it becomes a major priory.

To qualify as a simple priory the foundation must: (1) have six professed nuns ready to change stability and some novices coming to the end of their formation, (2) have sufficient buildings to make the regular life possible, and (3) have sufficient income to cover the important parts of the community's needs. All these requirements had been fulfilled, so it was easy for the General Chapter to promote Tautra Mariakloster to a simple priory. One significant issue in the visitation was their progress in inculturation, which included the community learning to speak Norwegian. The Sisters had a teacher who came, and the government paid for four hundred hours of class time. The course was completed, they can all read Norwegian, and most can carry on a conversation and read and write it. What they want to do now is use it more when they travel outside the monastery for shopping and so on. The liturgy is mostly in Norwegian, but the chapter talks and refectory readings three or four days a week are in English. They would like to start using Norwegian more, but it is difficult. Everyone in the country knows English very well, especially the young people. They start English classes in the third grade. I was talking to a college-age girl at the bus depot, and she said in high school and college they learn English from American TV shows, movies, and music. The sisters have a hard time sticking to Norwegian because if they get stuck over a word in a conversation with a Norwegian, the person goes into English right away.

One of the hardest things to get used to at Tautra was almost twenty-four hours of daylight in the summer time. The sun sets about 1:30 AM and rises at 3:00 AM and in between it is a period of twilight. It never really gets dark. The sun rises in the north and sets in the north, since this part of Norway is close to the Arctic Circle. So summers are all light and winters are all dark.

The architect chosen to design the new monastery was from Oslo, and he had built a few churches there. He liked to have little gardens brought into the building. There were about five to ten such gardens in the plan. One little wall section of the church, for example, is glass that overlooks a water garden. By the soap department, there is an herb garden. Outside the refectory is a vegetable garden. These gardens are enclosed by four walls but open to the sky. The whole monastery is about one hundred feet from the fjord.

The first chaplain of Tautra was recently elected abbot at Mellifont Abbey in Ireland. Presently, Fr. Anthony O'Brien, who hails from Kerry and joined Roscrea Monastery, serves as the nuns' chaplain. By way of geographical proximity, Tautra falls under the region of the Isles.

On March 25, 2006, the Tautra Mariakloster moved from the status of a foundation to a simple priory, and Mother Rosemary was elected the first prioress. In this way, it attains its independence of governance from the motherhouse, Our Lady of the Mississippi Abbey in Dubuque, although Mississippi Abbey continues to maintain some financial dependence as the need arises. Through the generosity of many benefactors, a complete monastery was constructed and was finished in August 2006.

The Fjords of Tautra Give Praise and Welcome[16]

Sometime in the 1100s St. Bernard of Clairvaux wrote a letter to Henry Murdock in which he says, "Believe me who has experience, you will find more laboring amongst the woods than you ever will amongst books. Woods and stones will teach you what you can never hear from any master" (Letter 107). Yesterday, sitting looking out at the fjord, I wondered if we could say the same about water. Does it teach like the woods and stones? What would the fjord tell us if it could speak?

Perhaps it would say to the sisters:

> We have been waiting for you. Welcome. We are here to care for you. We will heat your house in the winter and cool it in the summer. We will refresh you when you are thirsty and cleanse you at the end of the day. Nothing grows on the island without us. We are the nurturing springs from deep in the earth bringing healing waters, refreshing waters, and cleansing waters. But listen, we go back to the beginning. We watered the Garden of Eden. It is not even recorded when we were created. The land itself rose out of us. We covered the earth and receded at the command of the Creator.
>
> We remember the angel gliding over us on the Sea of Galilee on his mission to Nazareth. Then we knew why the psalmist

---

16. Homily given to the sisters' community at Tautra, Norway, on the occasion of the blessing and foundation of the new priory on March 25, 2006, the Solemnity of the Annunciation of the Lord.

called upon all of us, the waters of the deep, the waters above the heavens, all streams and water courses, to praise the Lord. It was the moment he took a body from the Virgin. We loved St. Bernard's use of the words, "and the Virgin's name was Mary." We whisper these words to you as you go by, "and the Virgin's name was Mary." Listen to us softly murmur this to you day and night. We never sleep. Just as Mary conceived him on this day, you conceived him in your spirit in baptism.

We were the water poured over you. From that moment your heart never sleeps either. For deep in the core of your being our Savior prays unceasingly like a hidden river within you saying: "Come to the Father."

We received the body of the Lord in the Jordan and were made holy that very day. The Lord uses us to bless you at the end of each day. We were even used today to bless the walls of your church and in a few minutes a drop of our water will be added to the chalice as a sign of the mingling of the human and divine at the Eucharist. Blood and water flowed from his side on the cross and out of this stream the Church was born.

We are so happy you are finally here. The Lord chose you for this place by our side from all creation. We are your elder sisters here to help you live the mystery of Jesus once again. We are "A strain of the earth's sweet being in the beginning" ("Spring," Gerard Manley Hopkins). We speak with many voices, listen to us.

Well, sisters, if the Creator uses water to come to us in so many ways, how much more will he use your new community, the very body of his Son Jesus? What a historic day for Norway! Your words of prayer will express the deep soul of all Norwegians, whether they are aware of it or not. For at the core of each person's being is the thirst for God. Your vocation is to represent this thirst by thirsting yourselves. You are to experience the words of Jesus on the cross: "I thirst." He is thirsting for our love. "If anyone thirst let him come to me; let him drink who believes in

me . . . from within him rivers of water shall flow" (John 7:37-38).
"Whoever drinks the water I give him . . . shall have a fountain
within leaping up to provide eternal life" (John 4:14). St. Bernard
used to love to repeat to his monks the words from Proverbs: "Be
the first to drink from your own well."

Sisters, you know and have tasted this river of living water
within you, this fountain leaping up to eternal life. You have
followed it to the source of your very being and there have come
face-to-face with your Creator, though it be night. I love the
words of St. Anselm: "I have been created to see God but I have
yet to do what I have been created to do." And even more the
words of St. Hilary: "I have a firm grasp on something I do not
understand." Your monastic life, your monastery, is a mystery.
No one fully understands it, but you have drunk deeply at the
spring within you. You know the depths of love at the core of
your life. You have sacrificed all for this one precious pearl found
only in the deepest waters of your soul. In this way you reveal
the essence of the human heart so that others may know that the
love of God is in their heart too. You carry everyone in your heart.
You may never see the fruits of your labor because we live by
faith, not by sight. But you are a mother and a sister to all humanity. You are the voice for those who do not know their own voice.
You are the cry going up from the ends of the earth to the
Father.

We call the ceremony about to be enacted a transfer of your
vow of stability. Sounds rather distant and abstract, does it not?
What it really means is that you are transferring your heart to
this place, to this safe island, to this monastery, to the people of
Norway. For the last seven years you have known the love of the
Norwegian people for you. Their presence here today means they
will not let you down. They will care for your heart and support
you.

My nephew, who recently became a father, sent me an in-
sightful quote that says, "Having a child . . . is to decide forever
to have your heart go walking around outside your body." This
community is your child, needing your care. Your heart is in it.

Jesus is the heart of the invisible God. His heart is in this community too. Together you form one person, Jesus in you and you in him.

Dear sisters, all the voices of the island are speaking to you today—the living and the dead, the monks who have gone before you, the good Christians who have lived here for centuries, the birds of the sky, the fish in the water, the community of all God's creatures sing the glad song of redemption: "With joy you will draw waters from the wells of salvation."

Chapter Two

CELEBRATIONS OF MONASTIC LIFE

We often speak of the differences between cultures. Without thinking too much about it, we know that the way things are done in the United States is not the way they are done in Japan or France. We have learned that it is wise to be aware of cultural differences when interacting with people from other countries and ethnic backgrounds.

Similarly, the monastery has its own culture, its own way of doing things, observances, norms, and rules of behavior. Examples can be found in the special customs and traditions we observe to mark important events in the life of a monk. The reception of the monastic habit, the profession of vows, and a monk's golden anniversary are all examples of important milestones in his life. These special occasions are celebrated within the context of the liturgy and often include a festive meal afterwards.

In this section we have gathered together a selection of remarks taken from a variety of liturgical contexts, chapter talks, and homilies which try to capture the essence of what is being celebrated.

RECEPTION OF THE NOVICE'S HABIT

For this rite, the community assembles in the chapter room. The novice director enters with the postulant, who prostrates before the abbot. The abbot says "rise in the name of the Lord," and when the community has expressed willingness to accept the postulant into the novitiate, one of the brothers reads from chapter 58 of the Rule of St. Benedict, "The Procedure for Receiving Brothers." Following the abbot's exhortation, the clothing of the new novice takes place. To conclude the ceremony, the abbot exchanges the sign of peace with the new novice.

Fulfilling the Law of Christ[17]

Paul, you have been with us several months now and hopefully you have experienced some of the peace of the monastic life. St. Benedict wants the monastery to be a place of peace. He does not want anyone unduly disturbed in the House of God. This is a key phrase, *Domus Dei*, the House of God. St. Benedict conceives of the monastery as a House of God where monks live in the sight of God. Guarding our hearts for the sake of mindfulness of God makes up a large portion of our monastic daily practice.

The way we live together should be a witness to all that we are aware of living in the House of God. There is no class distinction among us. We are "to be the first to show respect to the other" (RB 72:4), to be obedient to one another, and share everything in common. All this is based on our awareness of living in the presence of God, living in the House of God. Paul, you know and we all know that this awareness does not come easily. It is not natural for us to give in to the other. It is not natural for us to put others first.

There is a flip side to the monastic life and St. Benedict has many names for it: the hard and difficult things (*dura et aspera*, in Latin), humiliations, even the injustices. He calls our life in the monastery a battle, a hand-to-hand combat with the evil one. In other words, monastic life is going to be a struggle. St. Benedict is careful to say that the "novice should be clearly told all the hardships and difficulties that will lead him to God" (RB 58:9).

17. From the exhortation given to Paul Kronebusch (now named Br. Joseph) during the reception of the monastic habit on January 8, 2006, held in the abbey's chapter room.

I will not have time to list all the hardships and difficulties! Just believe me they will be there. Contrary to all appearances, they will not be put there deliberately! When I was a novice, I used to think the one in charge of work was deliberately testing me by assigning me to what I thought were the worst work assignments. You might run into some of this in years ahead; Paul, even though it is not planned, it is part of the picture. St. Benedict says we are to put up with weaknesses of mind and behavior, our own and others, not only to put up with them, but to bear each other's burdens and thus fulfill the law of Christ.

Fulfilling the law of Christ is what it is all about. So Paul, I can only paraphrase St. Benedict's wisdom when he says to the newcomers: do not bolt right away from the road that leads to life. Depend on God above and eventually your heart will expand, and you will understand more clearly the ways of the Lord.

The Deifying Light[18]

Nicholas, we began our morning prayer last Thursday with the ancient hymn, *Ecce Jam Noctis* which translates, "Lo, the dim shadows of the night are waning; radiantly glowing, dawn of day returns now."

These few words are a beautiful example of how nature can reflect the life of grace. It is like a beautiful sunrise—a glowing morning—a radiant beginning of day.

Nicholas, this is my wish for you as you begin your novitiate: may it be like a radiant dawn for you!

After we sang the hymn at Lauds on Thursday, we began the psalmody, and the mood changed dramatically with the words of Psalm 87: "In the morning my prayer comes before you. Wretched, close to death from my youth, I have borne your trials; I am numb."

18. From the exhortation given to Br. Nicholas Koenig on the occasion of his reception of the novice's habit on July 9, 2006, held at the abbey's chapter room.

The psalm ends on this somber note: "Friend and neighbor you have taken away: my one companion is darkness" (Ps 87:16, 19); here is the other side of the novitiate! It is actually the other side of the monastic life. We all experience periods of radiance and periods of darkness. I would even go so far as to say it is easier for us to describe the darkness than it is for us to explain the radiance.

St. Benedict tells the abbot to be sure and let the novice know about the *dura et aspera*—the hard and difficult things that lead to God. It is good to keep this last phrase in mind because we need to remember that hard and difficult things, if understood properly and accepted, can lead to God.

There are certain aspects of monastic life that are inherently difficult. For instance, you will not be able to totally control your living conditions or your physical environment because you are joining a community, where the common good usually comes first. In a certain way, Nicholas, you will even have to give up some of your personal ideals to the ideals of the community.

At times you may feel you are not being treated fairly. In describing the fourth degree of humility, St Benedict even goes so far as to say a monk may feel he is being unjustly treated. This happens in community life at times. You may feel misunderstood and not appreciated. I hope none of these things will happen, but they have happened to us all, and they are the times we may be tempted to give up. Later, however, often much later, we come to realize that the hard and difficult things lead to God. We are being dispossessed in order to be possessed by God. We die that we may live.

But the hard and difficult things are not the complete picture of our life. There is much radiance and joy. Benedict speaks of it as an "unspeakable sweetness" (RB Prol. 49). He says elsewhere that we live constantly in *aspectus divinitatis*, in the sight of God. If we could only open our eyes to the deifying light, and our ears to the one who loves us and calls to us daily: "See how the Lord in his love shows us the way to life" (RB Prol. 20).

Nicholas, you are entering a "school of the Lord's service" (Prol. 45), or as the Cistercian Fathers call it, "a school of love."

It is a school of transformation where we learn how to put on the mind of Christ.

What is needed for you now is to develop a personal relationship with the Lord Jesus because, as our Constitutions remind us, it is only out of this relationship that the gifts of our Cistercian vocation can flower (Cst. 3:5).

May the Lord bring to completion the work he has begun in you.

SOLEMN PROFESSION OF VOWS

One of the most joyful occasions for a monastic family is to celebrate a solemn profession. Almost every style of life or career has a time of initiation, probation, or training. In the monastery, we call it initial formation. It can last from a minimum of five years to ten years. At the end of this formative period, the young monk makes a formal petition to the abbot asking to make solemn vows. If the abbot agrees with the petition, he presents the candidate to the community for a vote. To be accepted, one must receive over half of the votes cast by the conventual chapter, that is, all the solemnly professed monks of the community. Solemn profession basically means a person is making a lifelong commitment to the monastic way of life.

Following is an explanation of the rite of solemn profession which takes place at the Eucharist in the abbey church, usually on a major feast day.

After the Gospel at Mass, the one to be professed is called from out of the community to the front of the altar. There the abbot asks the monk what he is seeking. The answer is always the same, "The mercy of God and the Order" (this means the Cistercian Order as represented by the community). The abbot then gives an exhortation—several are included in this chapter. The candidate is then asked a few ritualized questions about his intention and resolution. The community is then asked to pray for the one about to make vows. This prayer is either the sung *Veni, Creator Spiritus* ("Come, Holy Spirit") or the litany of the saints. While these prayers are being sung, the monk makes a full prostration on the floor of the church as an act of total humility and submission to God. Following this, the actual profession takes place when the monk reads the formula binding him by a solemn vow to a life of poverty, chastity, obedience, stability, and conversion of life. This formula is read in a loud voice for all to hear. The parchment is then signed on the altar and left there for the duration of the Mass. As a full member of the community, the new monk goes to each solemnly professed and kneels before him and begs his prayers, followed by the embrace of peace. Returning to the front of the altar, the newly professed prostrates again, while the abbot recites the long prayer of monastic consecration. This prayer is made to the Father and the Son and the Holy Spirit and officially consecrates one a monk in the Catholic Church. After the prayer, the newly professed receives as the sign of a monk the white cowl and returns to his place in choir; the Eucharist continues.

There is nothing said in the Rule of St. Benedict, but it has become a sacred custom to have a festive meal with the community and family and friends of the new monk.

Professing Love to the God of Love[19]

A "Freudian slip" has been defined as the slip of the tongue or pen that reveals a deep dark secret about what you are really thinking but do not want anyone to know. It may be something that you have been repressing. For example, if I started out by saying, "Dear servants and fiends," instead of "Dear Sisters and friends," the Sisters might say, "I knew it all along; he thinks we are his servants," and the guests would add, "He thinks we are fiends."

It can work the other way too. As I was preparing my notes for this homily I wrote at the top of the page, "Solemn Profession

19. Homily delivered at Our Lady of the Mississippi Abbey, Dubuque, Iowa, on the occasion of the solemn religious profession of Sr. Grace Remington, ocso, on June 11, 2005.

of St. Grace" instead of "Sr. Grace." There is only a one-letter difference between "Sr." and "St.," but there is a lifetime before a sister becomes a saint! It reminds me of T. S. Eliot's famous words, *"In my end is my beginning."* Beginnings are important, but how we end is the clincher. No one is a saint until the end. So I guess it is a little premature, Sr. Grace, to cross the "t" just yet.

"In my end is my beginning" is one of those great lines that can be used on many occasions. Poets have a gift for this, namely, to turn out phrases that can be taken out of context in order to shine a little light on our human experiences. One of my favorites is from Rilke. He says, *"We live our life forever taking leave."* I think of this often in that space of nostalgia after a friend leaves, or during a group meeting such as a General Chapter when everyone is gathering their suitcases to go home. After three weeks of intense working together with two hundred superiors from around the world, a bond is formed but we must take our leave perhaps never to meet again. In a way, Sr. Grace's friends might be feeling this way today. Sr. Grace is making a definitive decision to live a monastic way of life that removes her from certain family gatherings or vacations with friends. We are forever taking leave of things in this life until we are filled with life eternal.

Then there is the line from Yeats's poem "The Second Coming" which goes, *"The center cannot hold."* The original context was a poem about modern society, but the phrase fits all kinds of occasions. When you least expect them, these little poetic insights turn up in your mind to shed light on your experiences.

As I was looking over the readings Sr. Grace chose so carefully for her solemn profession, one of these poetic phrases jumped out at me. It can be taken out of context and applied to everyone's life. It is from the second reading in today's liturgy from St. Paul: "There must be love" (Col 3:14). How true. There must be love. To be truly human, our lives must have love. St. Paul says it binds everything together and completes the whole. Elsewhere he writes, "Without love I am nothing" (1 Cor 13:2).

Looking at the booklet that Sr. Grace put together and the readings she chose to express herself at this most important time of her life, you would have to say, "Here is a woman in love." Nothing more needs be said. I probably should end the homily here, but we must ask the question, what is love? St. Paul says it binds everything together. It completes life. Without it our lives are incomplete, not held together. *"The center cannot hold."* Love is the center of our lives. At the core of our being is Love. God is love and that is how we are the image and likeness of God. We must enter into the center of our own being to find the source of love. This cannot be forced, no more than we can force someone to love us. We must wait in patience for the door to open. As we wait, we serve the Lord with devotion.

St. Francis de Sales tells us that devotion is to love what luster is to a diamond. It is the brilliance of life. All the little ceremonies of solemn profession are shining from the heart of Sr. Grace, helping her to express her love.

Love, however, is not always glowing. Love means to care, and if we care, we are vulnerable, open to pain, open to having our hearts broken at times.

Sr. Grace chose as her first reading the beautiful words of the prophet Hosea: "So I will allure her; I will lead her into the desert and speak to her heart" (Hos 2:16). In Hosea, this passage refers to the exodus of the slaves out of Egypt. The prophets saw the exodus as a time of intimacy with the Lord. It was sort of a golden period that formed the thinking of Israel for all times. "I will bring her into the wilderness and speak tenderly to her," says the Lord. Yet, in the book of Deuteronomy, the author saw the exodus as a time of testing: "God led you for forty years in the desert, to humble you, to test you and know your inmost heart" (Deut 8:2). Monastic life has both of these elements: intimacy with the Lord and testing by the Lord to reveal the inmost heart. This fits with today's Gospel about pruning the vine to produce more fruit (John 15:1-12). St. Benedict warns those who take up the monastic life that they must pass through many "hard and difficult things" before arriving at the type of love that casts out fear. And so it is for us, and so it will be for Sr. Grace.

So what is love? It is many things. It is like the facets of a diamond that bring out the beauty of the gem. Love is service, love is intimacy, love is fidelity under testing, love does not give up, love is surrender, and love is caring. These are facets of love. The facets of a diamond bring out its luster but they are not the essence. A diamond receives light and reflects light that is transformed into many colors inside the diamond. So it is with a human being. At the heart of a person is love. She receives love and gives love. All the facets of love reflect the center of the person. There we find love. Our human love is transformed into divine love as we journey toward the end that is our beginning.

Commenting on words similar to Our Lord's in today's Gospel where Jesus says, "Abide in me as I abide in you," St. John of the Cross writes, "In the transformation of love each gives possession of self to the other, and each leaves and exchanges self for the other. Thus each one lives in the other and is the other, and both are one in the transformation of love" (*The Spiritual Canticle* 12.7).

So what is love? God is love.

Community—the Word of Salvation[20]

When someone comes to join the monastery, one of the things we are supposed to find out is if this person is truly seeking God, or if he is here for other reasons. Br. Paul Andrew, you have been with us seven years now, and during this time, we have come to believe that to the best of our knowledge, you are truly seeking God in our way of life.

The ritual this morning, the solemn profession of your vows, is an official validation, a kind of stamp of approval, an authentication of your vocation. Of course only God can see into your heart. We can only see externals, but from them we can conclude

20. Homily delivered at the abbey church on the Solemn Feast of Christ the King on the occasion of the solemn profession of vows by Br. Paul Andrew Tanner, ocso, on November 20, 2005.

there is something motivating you beyond what we can see, perhaps even beyond what you can see. It is the hidden call, the desire placed in your heart that motivates you to stand up before this assembly and proclaim that you are freely choosing this monastic way to God. We have observed you over the past several years rising for Vigils at 3:15 A.M.; we see you every day helping our infirm brothers and bearing patiently, as St. Benedict teaches, the weaknesses of body and character that we all experience. It is now time for us to say, yes, you are one of us. You are our brother.

Our Cistercian Fathers taught that the first step in becoming a monk, the first movement in formation, the first foundation on which the whole edifice of your future monastic life is built, is self-knowledge. I have found out the hard way, as all of us probably have, that this first step is not learned in a few years. It is a long process. Earlier I quoted St. Benedict as having said we are to "support with the greatest patience, one another's weaknesses of body and character" (RB 72:5). We cannot begin to do this unless we bear patiently our own weaknesses of body and character. This is the beginning of self-knowledge, the beginning of wisdom. We can be compassionate to others only when we are compassionate to ourselves.

When I was reading over today's Gospel about the last judgment (Matt 25:31-46), I saw those to be condemned remarking to the Lord, "Lord, when did we see you hungry, or thirsty or away from home or naked or ill or in prison and did not attend to your needs?" Two things came to my mind. One was how the people in the Gospel story lacked true self-knowledge, and second, how dangerous our monastic life can be if we are not in touch with ourselves. We come here to truly seek God. We emphasize prayer, *lectio*, solitude, silence, and giving up our selfish ways. We can pursue all these things with single-minded zeal and forget that we are living with others. The condemned ones in today's Gospel were shocked. They thought of themselves as good people. They would have certainly attended to the Lord if they saw him on their journey through life, but they never recognized him. They did see some people in need, some sick people, some prisoners, some down-and-outers, but they had their eyes set on God, not on these needy people. Their single-minded zeal misdirected them. No one is condemned without a chance. They must have had an inkling that God was present in the needy, but they did not expect to find him there. Maybe they refused to see God in such poor conditions.

How we live in community shows what kind of monks we really are inside. The monastery is like a small world within the larger world of society. We have everything we need for salvation. This can be said of all people. Everyone lives in the small world of their families, their neighborhoods or parish churches, their workplaces. None of us operates on a global level. Gandhi was once asked how to bring about world peace. Bring peace to your own heart was his reply. This advice can serve us all. How you live in your limited world has unlimited influence for the good of all. We have been able to document how individuals changed the course of history, but in the realm of salvation history things are more hidden. Whose prayers are sustaining me or who is being helped by my prayers is a mystery. An act of kindness to a stranger can determine the course of your eternity. A hidden prayer can give someone the courage to go on.

Today's Gospel is not so much a parable of the last judgment as much as a parable about how our eternity is related to our daily life. The ones who truly sought God during their journeys through life are the ones who sought to see him in every circumstance of their lives. If we lose this perspective, the monastery can be a dangerous place. We can appear to be truly seeking God when in fact we miss his true presence among us. We have a lot of spiritual practices in the monastery. In fact St. Benedict outlines seventy-seven of them for us in chapter 4 of the Rule, "The Instruments of Good Works." After enumerating them, he says, "The work-shop where we should work hard at all these things is the monastic enclosure and stability in the community" (RB 4:78). Br. Paul, you are about to profess a vow of stability to this community. We welcome you with open arms. In ancient times young monks used to ask the seniors for a word of salvation. If I can presume to take the role of a senior, my word to you is "community." This is where you will work out your salvation. This is where you will attain true self-knowledge. This is where you will find God.

Love Never Ends[21]

The liturgy today is all about beginnings; the beginning of our Cistercian Order and the beginning of your life, Jonah, as a solemnly professed monk of New Melleray. All religious congregations were advised to go back to their beginnings and from that pristine place start the process of renewal. For us, that means going back to our founders in the year 1098. The further we go back in history the harder it is to determine how a movement, such as the Cistercian Order, began. There are multiple interpretations of what exactly Sts. Robert, Alberic, Stephen, and their eighteen companions set out to achieve by moving from Molesme to Citeaux. They were already monks in the Benedictine mode of Cluny. Why did they want to leave their monastery to go to what has been described as the wilderness of Citeaux? Behind all the interpretation there is the one fact: they wanted a more authentic expression of the monastic ideal.

We do know that in the golden age of the Order our Cistercian Fathers called the monastery a school of love. They wrote eloquently about the art of love. Jonah, in the readings you chose for your profession day, this theme of love is prominent. In the Gospel, Jesus tells us love sums up the law and the prophets, in other words, the whole Scriptures: "You shall love the Lord your God with your whole heart, with your whole soul and with all your mind" (Matt 22:37). Paul goes so far as to say faith and hope will end but love never ends (1 Cor 12:7-8; 13:13). It is the one thing that crosses over with us to the other shore.

---

21. Homily delivered at the abbey church on the Solemn Feast of Sts. Robert, Alberic, and Stephen, the founders of Citeaux, to celebrate the solemn profession of Br. Jonah Wharff on January 26, 2006.

Love never ends. Can we ask when it begins? Can any of us remember when love began for us? Perhaps some people can pinpoint a given moment when they fell in love, but falling in love is more like an awakening than a beginning. When did love begin for each of us? I do not think we know. This question comes from an experience I had recently while watching a young couple with their newborn infant. Love was pouring out of the parents for their new daughter. She will not remember a thing about these early months of her life, and yet, she has been receiving love and will be able to give love in return. Somewhere in her little psyche, the core of her being, in her heart, love has been imprinted. This place is deeper than her memory. What has happened here in the depth of her being will continue to happen and it will never be forgotten. We might say that love began for each of us with our parents, but then when did it begin for them? If we trace it back to its origins we have to conclude that love began with God because God is love. No one is born without a spark of God's love in them. It is what it means to be created in the image and likeness of God.

The paradox is that we possess this ability to love but often forget where it came from. There are a couple of powerful images in the readings Jonah chose that are based on sight but really refer to our lack of spiritual awareness. One represents those who are totally out of it; the other refers to the rest of us. About the clueless, Sirach says they are like an eye with no pupil: "When the pupil of the eye is missing there is no light" (Sir 3:24). He is not referring to physical blindness, but the type of blindness Helen Keller spoke of when she said it is a terrible thing to be born blind, but it is altogether worse to have eyes and not see. An eye without a pupil by analogy is a heart without love, human beings without the awareness of who they are.

The other image applies to all of us. St Paul says that even the most aware perceive spiritual things in a confused manner: "We see indistinctly as in a mirror" (1 Cor 13:12). He says this because we can go through life blinded to what is really important. Love is to the monastic life what the pupil is to the eye. In everything we do, Paul says, we have to be motivated by love otherwise we are nothing but clanging cymbals and noisy gongs (1 Cor 13:1).

Br. Jonah, you are entering the school of love. You once told me you made a resolution to always respond to whatever service you are asked to perform for the community. Your model is the Lord himself, who came among us to serve and not to be served. Humble service is a form of love; it leads to spiritual awareness. Humble service is perhaps the most difficult success to achieve; it brings knowledge and wisdom not of this world.

St. Benedict and our Cistercian Fathers speak of the spiritual senses, the ears of the heart and the eyes of the soul. They are referring to a type of spiritual awareness that is beyond our control. It is a gift. It comes after years of fidelity or after years of loving service in the Church. The eye of the soul lets the light of Christ illumine our whole being. For the monk, the pupil of this eye is love expressed in humble service to the community.

The self-giving you are about to express in your vows, Br. Jonah, will be lived out in your daily monastic life of service. In your initial years with us, you have proven yourself true. My prayer is that the Lord will complete the good work he has begun in you.

TRANSFER OF STABILITY

It is not unheard of that a monk or nun transfers from one monastery to another. Our holy founders, Robert, Alberic, and Stephen did just that. They and their eighteen fellow monks left Molesme and founded a monastery at Citeaux in France. Thus began the Cistercian Order. To this day individuals have been doing this. In our modern times this means there is usually a liturgy comparable to that of solemn profession where in fact only the vow of stability is transferred. The next three homilies were given on such an occasion.

The Cowl as the Garment of Salvation[22]

There is a very symbolic moment in today's ceremony when Sr. Anne will be clothed in the white Cistercian cowl. The cowl will be taken from the altar, and Mother Gail will put it on Sr. Anne.

I suspect this ritual was in Sister's mind when she chose the first reading: "I rejoice heartily in the Lord, in my God is the joy of my soul; For he has clothed me with a robe of salvation and wrapped me in a mantle of justice" (Isa 61:10). The prophet Isaiah is referring to being wrapped in garments of salvation.

Indeed, today Sr. Anne is being clothed; she is not clothing herself. It is fitting that the important people in her life are here this morning to witness this event. One of them is her mother; the first to clothe her and care for her. It is also significant that the members of her Benedictine community have joined us here today because they are the ones who first gave her the religious habit. Finally, her Cistercian community is present for this ceremony to witness the abbess clothe her in the white cowl.

When you clothe someone, it implies that you will care for that person. A mother clothes an infant and cares for her. The Benedictine community gave Sister an exceptional opportunity to learn the Sacred Scriptures, and now her Cistercian community has taken on the responsibilities of her education in the school of charity.

All of these actions, especially the one today, symbolize our being clothed with Christ. It means putting on the new person, being conformed to Christ, and taking on the mission of Christ. Our Cistercian founders wanted to be poor with the poor Christ, not just for the sake of poverty. They understood this as a way of coming closer to Christ, a way of identifying with him. In wearing the cowl of a monk, they were saying what monks have said since the time of St. Anthony: we embrace our human condition because Jesus emptied himself and took the form of a slave.

22. Homily delivered on the transfer of stability for Sr. Anne Elizabeth Sweet, ocso, at Our Lady of the Mississippi Abbey on January 25, 2001.

Our cowl has this twofold symbolism. It is a garment of salvation, a wedding garment, hence, a festal attire; and it is a garment of the penitent as it is shaped in the form of a cross. It conforms us to the sufferings of Christ.

There is a phrase that comes up in the document we call the "Little Exordium," an account of how Citeaux was founded. It is a principle all monks and nuns can follow: "Cistercian monks should pursue the etymology of their name" (*Exordium Parvum* 15:6). In other words, if we stick close to the word "monk" and live like a monk, we will not wander far from our roots. But as you know, the word has many meanings. I would like to take two of these meanings and join them with the second and third readings of our liturgy this morning.

First of all, the Greek word *monos* means one, that is, united, complete, unified, whole. This is the fullness Jesus talks about after the great renunciation of leaving all things: the hundredfold. The symbolism of the cowl here refers to the union of Christ and Sr. Anne. In our Cistercian tradition, it is the union of the bride and the bridegroom. St. Bernard says, "Although none of us would dare to call ourselves the Bride of Christ, nevertheless we are members of the Church which rightly boasts the title and the reality it signifies" (St. Bernard, *On the Songs*, sermon 12:11). No one can live the monastic life very long without tasting some of this hundredfold.

Another meaning of the word "monk" is similar yet different: one, alone, single, solitary, separated, and even isolated. Monastic life also includes these kinds of experiences, those of the desert. Our second reading from Hebrews says it well in speaking of our ancestors: "They were only strangers and nomads on earth (Heb 11:13-14)." People who use such terms about themselves make it quite plain they are in search of a homeland.

Living like this as strangers in search of a home makes us vulnerable and insecure. In putting on the monastic cowl, we are embracing the cross, the trials and struggles of the monastic life. To be poor with the poor Christ has many meanings (cf. Mark 10:24b-30).

Sr. Anne, you are not changing course in the middle of your journey. You are simply moving from one Benedictine family tradition to another. As St. Benedict says, we go all together into eternal life (RB 72:12).

And we will one day be numbered with those who "died before receiving any of the things promised, but they saw them in the distance" (Heb 11:13).

We live with the certainty of faith and with the insecurity of faith; only faith can prove the existence of realities unseen.

Continuing Journey to Union with Christ[23]

Small children are known to have vivid imaginations. They are able to live in a fantasy world for long periods of time, and for a while they cannot distinguish fact from fantasy. They can have imaginary playmates, or friends who keep them company and conveniently get blamed for their misbehavior. Even as adults we are tempted to think this way. I know a middle-aged woman who rationalizes her bad behavior by making a distinction between the "good Ann" and the "bad Ann."

We grow out of this fantasy thinking eventually, but we never grow out of the root of this thinking, the divided self. It is something we struggle with all our lives. Spiritual writers speak of the true self and the false self. Today's Gospel says, "God did not send the Son [Spirit] into the world [flesh] to condemn the world but that the world might be saved through him" (John 3:17). Scripture talks of the flesh and the spirit. St. Paul refers to our old nature and our new nature—or, as it once was translated, "the old man and the new man." It reminds me of a story about an abbot who was presiding at the solemn profession of one of the sisters from a nearby monastery. He had changed the words to fit the gender, and so when he came to the prayer about the old and new man he substituted the word woman—"May the

---

23. Homily delivered at the abbey church on the occasion of the transfer of stability for Fr. Alberic Farbolin, ocso, on September 14, 2003.

Lord drive out the old woman in you. . . ." Afterwards, the abbess accused him of talking about her!

We all have to live with a divided self, but we yearn for a united self. For some reason, we believe that to achieve union with ourselves, we have to live at a higher plain of existence. We have to deny a lower self—our bodily self, our humiliated self, our suffering self—to live at a higher level, above the turmoil and confusion of life at a place where nothing mundane can touch us. There are many teachers to lead us on the journey upwards, and St. Paul calls this teaching the wisdom of the world. Opposed to it is the wisdom of the cross. The mysterious hymn in Paul's letter to the Philippians we heard this morning explains it like this: "[Jesus] emptied himself, taking the form of a slave, becoming as human beings are, and being in every way like a human being, he was humbler yet, even to accepting death, death on a cross" (Phil 2:7-8). As Christians, we embrace this path of descent into the suffering of life so that the pattern of the cross may be the pattern of our life for the sake of the glory it will bring.

Today we have the example of one who professes his faith in this journey of the cross. Fr. Alberic Farbolin is transferring his vow of stability to New Melleray. It is a nuance because the essence of his life is not changed. He is a monk, one who aspires to be undivided, a whole person. He is on the journey, and we are happy to have him as our brother.

St. Benedict teaches us how to walk this journey in what he calls the steps of humility. Chapter 7, "On Humility," is the heart of his Rule. We, like Jesus, descend in order to ascend. The twelve steps of humility provide us with a specific course of action to follow in order to put on the mind of Christ. In this journey nothing is left behind, nothing is condemned that is truly human. God so loved this world that he sent his only Son to save the world, not to condemn it.

The world is everything in nature, above all, our human nature. Jesus became human to save all things. Sometimes, when we have put a lot of effort into doing something with little results to show for it, we say, "Let it go; it is not worth saving." In our deeper life, our essence, nothing should be lost. Indeed, all will be redeemed through the cross of Christ.

This morning we will witness a man recommitting himself to following Jesus in the monastic way of life. As we participate in this ceremony, I suggest we all renew our own commitment to Christ in whatever way of life we have chosen.

Stability Means Home Where God-Is-With-Us[24]

> "Wherever you go, I will go, wherever you live I shall live" (Ruth 1:16).

To me these words are some of the most beautiful and touching in the Bible. They express such heartfelt emotions of friendship and fidelity. They are heart words. They remind me of Cardinal Newman's motto: *Cor ad cor loquitur* (heart speaks to heart). The words have strong appeal because they express a level of friendship we all long to experience.

When I was reflecting on the feeling behind these words, as well as the context in which they were first spoken and are now spoken, it occurred to me that we are never strangers when we are with someone we love. We can all see ourselves as a Ruth, as well as the foreigner who returned to thank Jesus, and also as sons and daughters of the patriarchs who set out in search of a homeland. All three of these models had a love burning in their hearts that led them through many difficulties. I am reminded of the words of St. John of the Cross: "I went without discerning and with no other light except for that which in my heart was burning."[25] You are never a stranger when you are with someone you love.

Recall the original context of Ruth's words. They were spoken when her mother-in-law *Naomi*, which means "sweetness,"

24. Homily delivered at Our Lady of the Mississippi Abbey on March 30, 2005.

25. *St. John of the Cross: Poems*, trans. Roy Campbell, "The Dark Night," stanza 3 (Baltimore: Penguin Books, 1960).

wanted to change her name to *Mara,* which means "bitterness" (Ruth 1:20). Her life was going south, as they say. It was spiraling downward. After professing her love, Naomi's other daughter-in-law decided to leave. Her name was *Orpah,* which means "she who turns away." Only Ruth, which means *"beloved,"* said she would stay behind with her mother-in-law, and she said it so beautifully: "Wherever you go, I will go, wherever you live, I shall live."

I think in these four people and their symbolic names, we have a microcosm of community life. We have days that are sweet and days that are bitter. We have days when people seem to turn away from us, and days that are filled with love. It seems to me the change of stability is about community life. It is about finding a home, a place where you can express love and receive love. We are reading the Vatican document "Fraternal Life in Community" in refectory right now. It mentions that living in community means "being responsible for each other's growth" (FLC, no. 24). We do not think about this very much, but we are responsible for each other's growth. No one is going to grow in a hostile environment or even in an indifferent environment. To care for each other is what it is all about, but when we care, we are going to suffer. It is easy to be tolerant when we do not care. We are each shepherds of growth for the other. When our life turns from Naomi to Mara, sweetness to bitterness, we need someone to be a Ruth to us, someone who will reach out a helping hand.

Symbolic names frequently show up in the Bible. Of course, the greatest is *Emmanuel,* a name that means "God is with us." So I think we can take Ruth's words and put them on the lips of Jesus in order to hear him say to each of us, "Wherever you go, I will go, wherever you live, I will live, and wherever you die, I will die." Jesus has embraced our human nature and has lived it to the limits. He has died our death and raised it up. I like the phrase St. Benedict uses when he refers to our life as the "humility of this present life" (RB 7:5). Humility is our ladder to heaven. Jesus has shown us the way. "See how the Lord in his love shows us the way of Life" (RB Prol. 20).

The humility of this present life in the monastery can challenge us. But we have the consolation of the Lord coming to us through the community. And we have the intimate voice of Jesus saying to us, "Wherever you go I will go. I will never leave you."

GOLDEN JUBILEE

In our twenty-first century, when men are joining the monastery later in life, we will have very few golden anniversaries. After the Second World War, many young veterans turned to religious life to find their true vocation. Now those who entered in the late 1940s and 1950s are celebrating their golden anniversary of monastic profession.

This is a very simple ceremony but a very touching one. The senior monk comes forward and reads aloud his profession formula, renewing his vows of poverty, chastity, obedience, stability, and conversion of life. He has been living these for fifty years and now renews them in front of the whole community.

The ceremony ends with the abbot giving the senior a wooden staff to help him in the last leg of his journey.

A Great Life Spent in Humility and Hiddenness[26]

Greatness is sometimes hidden in humble packages. Albert Einstein did not speak until he was four years old and could not read until age seven. His teacher called him "mentally slow and adrift in foolish dreams." The famous French sculptor, Rodin, who carved that great work of art called "The Thinker," was described by his father as an idiot. Three times he failed to gain admittance into art school. Beethoven's teacher said he was "hopeless" as a composer. Winston Churchill suffered a lifetime of setbacks, starting when he failed sixth grade. Rudyard Kipling

---

26. Homily delivered on the occasion of the golden jubilee celebration of Br. Walter Schoenberg, ocso, on March 19, 1999, the Feast of St. Joseph, at the New Melleray Church.

was rejected by the *San Francisco Examiner* with the comment, "You just do not know how to use the English language." Like all of these so-called losers who went on to such stunning success, St. Joseph must have considered himself a loser. First, he was faced with the trauma of realizing Mary was pregnant, and later, he was unable to protect the child Jesus except by fleeing his homeland with Mary and the child to become refugees in Egypt. His contemporaries would have laughed at him if he had told them about his dreams.

Joseph took Mary into his home. She bore a son, and Joseph named him Jesus. An ordinary carpenter, a devout wife, and a child. It was a family hardly worth noticing, unless you knew that the boy was the Son of God, and Joseph's wife was the Mother of God and would become Queen of the Universe, and Joseph himself was the guardian of God incarnate and of the Church that is the very Mystical Body of Christ. Their greatness was hidden in humble packages.

Nor did anyone sit up and take notice when a youthful twenty-two year old lad of German descent came to join New Melleray in August of 1946. Two-and-a-half years later, Br. Walter made his first profession of vows on March 19, 1949, the Feast of St. Joseph. Fifty years have passed. Today the Cistercian Order and the Church itself breaks silence in order to take notice of Walter's fidelity. We celebrate his continuing perseverance in a life entirely dedicated to prayer and to service of his brothers in community. It is a jubilee, which means "a shout of joy." Even the season of Lent is interrupted so that we may celebrate the Solemnity of St. Joseph and Walter's fiftieth anniversary.

Br. Walter, your life has something in common with the life of St. Joseph. St. Joseph was probably quite a young man when he took Mary into his home. Rabbis at the time of Christ taught that men should be married between the ages of thirteen and nineteen.[27] Our mental images of St. Joseph as an older man with

27. *New Catholic Encyclopedia*, vol. 7 (Washington, DC: Catholic University of America, 1967), 1107, no. 1.

streaks of gray running through his beard come from the art of medieval painters. They did not think that a youthful, handsome lad would be put in the same house as a virgin consecrated to God. But in the catacombs Joseph is always shown as a young beardless man, hardly much older than Mary. To these two youngsters, the Savior of the world was entrusted. And like the Savior they lived their lives in virginity, following a path that neighbors would have ridiculed if they had known about it. Chastity, virginity, and celibacy are not popular virtues in our culture today. But in the theology of John Cassian, the pursuit of chastity is the centerpiece of monastic asceticism because it prepares us for contemplation. That is why we take notice, and raise a shout of joy on the fiftieth anniversary of your profession of vows. Your vow of chastity, Br. Walter, is a gift that likens you to St. Joseph.

You have something else in common with him: poverty and heavy responsibilities. You had to take on responsibility early in life. Leaving school at the tender age of twelve, you helped your brother Victor run the family farm after the death of your father in the middle of the Great Depression. You experienced poverty and hard work, milking cows by hand, and plowing fields behind four horses, or five if the ground was hard. That extra horsepower made a big difference. And when you came of age, following the example of your older brother, Fr. Martin, you entered the Crosier Fathers (I have heard you say there was a secret motive in your heart. You wanted to escape the sweat and tears of farming in those difficult years). But you did not escape it, because five years later, when you joined New Melleray, the Lord, who has a sense of humor, and who is our true novice master, put you to work on the monastery farm and at our dairy barn.

Like St. Joseph the Worker, your life manifests the value of manual labor. Monks ought to live by the work of their own hands. At the age of seventy-five, when most people have been retired for many years, you continue to serve the community by caring for the sick in our infirmary. The three brothers you take care of also live in humble packages. What is more humbling than being in a wheelchair all day, dependent on others? But there is tremendous greatness in those three monks and in the brothers who care for them. We thank you for your labors of love, year in and year out, for over half a century. For this the Cistercian Order, the Church, and everyone here present raises a shout of joy.

We are encouraged by your example. We know that within the humble package that forms the envelope of your life on earth, there exists a greatness that comes from God, a greatness that will only be seen in all its splendor when we are gathered together in the kingdom of heaven. There it will be seen what a stunning success your life has been. May God keep you in holiness and bless you all the days of your life!

Now, let us bless our new jubilarian and witness the renewal of Br. Walter's vows.

Immaculate Conception and Fifty Years of Hidden Life in God[28]

As I was preparing my reflections for today, I got an idea from a little newspaper called *The Catholic Agitator*, published by the Catholic Worker House in Los Angeles. I love that name—*The Catholic Agitator*. Right away, it grabs your attention, it agitates you. It sets out to comfort the afflicted, and afflict the comfortable. The format of the newspaper and the name alone do that; even if you never read a word, you walk away angry. It did its job.

In the current issue of the newspaper, an article entitled "The Rock of Jesus" states that we are selling out to the god of materialism, the god of measurement, the god of quantification, and the god of technique. This is nothing new. Our scientific worldview has been around for a long time. It is the foundation of the way we think. It makes it difficult for us to believe in anything we cannot see or measure or quantify. Many changes in the Church have subtly been influenced by this scientific perspective.

---

28. Homily delivered on the Solemnity of the Immaculate Conception at New Melleray Church on the occasion of the golden jubilee celebration of Br. Felix Leja, ocso, on December 9, 2002.

For instance, the typical hagiography of the saints can leave us unmoved. What appeals to us is the humanness of the saints. We want to know that they were like us, not remote and distant.

Yet, having just said this, I need to retract it. I've never entered a Catholic church and found statues of the saints standing on the floor at eye level. I think it would be disconcerting. It would not feel right to walk up to a statue of St. Francis or St. Therese and be able to meet them eye-to-eye. It would be too familiar! For all our claims to be modern, we know instinctively that we do not want to see the saints standing on the floor. We want their feet about five feet off the ground, so we can look up at them. Our saints belong on pedestals.

This tells us they are remote, untouchable, unattainable, and approachable only on our knees. Almost instinctively we know there is something sacred about their lives. It is something we cannot touch, a hidden quality we can only approach on bended knees.

If this is true of the saints, how much more true of Mary the Mother of God, especially under the title of "The Immaculate Conception." That Mary was conceived without sin is something we would never know unless it was revealed. Follow her life through the Sacred Scriptures. She is a real mother, pondering things in her heart, perplexed at the absence of her son, sorrowful at the foot of the cross. Her Immaculate Conception did not shield her from life, but it was the hidden holiness of her life. It comes from the grace of her Son's redemption. It is a grace we all share. There is in each of our lives a remoteness, a hidden grace, or a redemption being played out daily as we respond to the Lord. We are not immaculately conceived, but we are conceived in grace at our baptism.

Today as we celebrate Mary's Immaculate Conception, we also honor one of our brother monks. Br. Felix Leja is celebrating his fiftieth year of profession—December 8, 1952, to December 8, 2002. There is nothing in his life to bedazzle us. But during those years of his monastic life, from 1952 to 2002, something sacred has always been there. The sacredness of his life has been hidden in God, remote, untouchable even by Br. Felix himself, yet present, waiting to be revealed.

Sr. Kitty Lawlor speaks of Mary Francis Clarke, founder of the Sisters of Charity of the Blessed Virgin Mary, in these words, "She knew in her heart what was right." This applies eminently to Mary, because from the moment of her conception her heart was right. In every event of her life she was guided by her heart, her immaculate heart. In her deepest joys and sufferings she knew in her heart what was right.

After fifty years, Br. Felix knows in his heart what is right. He can look back on more than fifty years and see that his heart, united in the Sacred Heart, has always guided him to what is true and right.

Chapter Three

CELEBRATIONS IN COMMUNITY LIFE

St. Pachomius (292–348) is the Father of Cenobitic (community) monasticism. Against his will, he was drafted into the army, and as a recruit, he was deeply moved by the kindness of the local Christians to the servicemen. Their care and love against a backdrop of the rudeness and roughness of army life moved him so deeply that after leaving the army, he became a Christian. He eventually became a monk and founded a monastery in Tabennisi on the Nile (Egypt), where he wrote a Rule for his community. Most monks at this time were hermits or semi-hermits. Complete community living was relatively new, and Pachomius was a pioneer on how to live as a monk in common. One of the main advantages of community life is mutual support and opportunities for fraternal charity.

The early monks always looked back to the description of the first Christian community as described in the Acts of the Apostles as their ideal: "Those who believed shared all things in common; they would sell their property and goods, dividing everything on the basis of each one's needs" (Acts 2:44). "The community of believers was of one heart and one mind. None of them ever claimed anything as his own; rather, everything was held in common" (4:32).

We speak of community living as the "common life." In the monastery, by virtue of the vow of poverty, no one owns anything; everything is held in common. This includes not only material goods, but also such things as intellectual gifts and talents of all kinds. We are not allowed to be stingy with our feelings and our thoughts. To live in community is to share your life as deeply as you are able with your brothers.

St. Benedict was a genius at organization. His monasteries are well ordered and pleasant places to live. The structure of the day is clearly laid out. To "live under a rule and an abbot" means to live in security and in deep peace. This is not simply due to Benedict's care in laying out the boundaries of each day; it goes much deeper than that. Benedict understands the psychology of living together. The strong are to help the weak; great hospitality is shown to the guest "as if they were Christ himself" (RB 53); the old are cared for and the young given special attention.

St. Benedict wants everything regulated so the "strong have something to strive for and the weak nothing to run from" (RB 64:19). The brothers "should each try to be the first to show respect to the other, supporting with the greatest patience one another's weakness of body or behavior" (RB 72:4-5).

These are the ideals of our common life. They come to us from the Acts of the Apostles, through St. Pachomius and St. Benedict, and give meaning to our life. Several years ago, there was a song by John Lennon, one of the Beatles, called "Imagine." Just imagine if the world adopted the ideals of cenobitic monastic life, even a fraction of them. Would it not be a better place to live?

Following are some talks dealing with the spiritual dimensions of everyday community living.

THE GIFT OF COMMUNITY LIFE

Living in Community

In June 2005, the BBC (British Broadcasting Company) produced a television series about the Benedictine monks of Worth Abbey in England. The program captured the experiences of five laymen as they lived the monastic life for forty days. Removed from their individualistic and materialistic society, they were able to seek out their deepest values and truest selves, quite possibly for the first time. Later that year the program's producer visited New Melleray to talk about the possibility of making an American version of the BBC documentary. She felt the documentary as shown in England valued monastic life and provided a counter-cultural model for people who want to live life at a deeper level, deeper than what modern culture has to offer. The community was split on whether we should get involved in making such a documentary in America, so without strong support, which would be needed for such an enterprise, we decided not to host the program. But we did give it serious consideration and in doing so raised this question: "What does the monastic life have to offer the world or the Church or the individual who joins one of our communities?"

By way of an answer, let me focus on the individual who joins a community.

First of all, the monastic life offers a person the opportunity to live in a stable community. The notion of "stability" is a rare entity, even in religion today. It is hard to achieve by yourself. Community is our support, but it is a great challenge to our individualistic way of thinking. We are all children of our American culture, and individualism is part of the air we breathe. Living an authentic community life pulls us out of ourselves; it is a way of dying to self and living for others.

This might seem to be a purely psychological observation, but the Christian community and monastic community are truly theological realities based on what it means to live out the mystery of the Body of Christ. We are members, one of the other, made one in Christ. Unity in the bond of charity is the goal of the Eucharist, which is the source of unity in the Church.

On a personal level, the monastic vocation offers us something very radical. It offers us ourselves. This may sound strange, but having a sense of who we are at the deepest level of our being is no easy matter.

St. Bernard says the first thing those who enter the monastery must do is learn to know themselves. This can be a painful process. To be called by God is to be touched by God. Our response, in all sincerity, is the one Peter gave when Jesus touched him: "Depart from me, Lord, for I am a sinful man" (Luke 5:8). But Jesus does not depart from Peter or from us. On the contrary, he invites us to follow him, to come along with him on his journey. Along the way, we will find our true identity. This is a lifelong process of finding ourselves in the Lord Jesus. It is the mystery of Jesus revealing the mystery of our own selfhood.

Recently we listened to a beautiful reading from St. Leo the Great at Vigils: "Mercy itself wishes you to be merciful . . . so that the Creator may shine forth in his creature, and the visage of God be reflected in the mirror of the human heart" (Liturgy of the Hours, 23rd Sunday of the Year). Similarly, St. Gregory of Nyssa teaches that our hearts have been covered over, obscured by sin. Once a life of virtue begins to take hold, and we begin living the Beatitudes, the debris is cleared away, the dirt from the mirror is washed clean, and our hearts reflect who we truly are: the image of God. Through a life of prayer this image is slowly revealed to us.

Prayer opens the door of our heart. Prayer brings us to the place where we dwell with God. Prayer then ceases to be our prayer, and becomes the prayer of Jesus to the Father. Our prayer and his prayer become one.

The monastic life is a journey from painful self-knowledge to the liberation of our spirit, our soul, or our image of God, which we believe in faith is our truest self.

Unifying Power of the Eucharist

Community is a very important part of our monastic life. In fact, the two polarities of our life are community and solitude. When someone applies to enter our monastery, we hope to see in him some potential for being able to live both in the community and in solitude. Not wholly one or the other but a balance of both.

Because grace builds on nature, we cannot bypass a person's natural talents, but they do not give us the full picture. We are a faith community; this adds a dimension to our life that is unseen and therefore presents a challenge to our perception of each other.

We meet each other everyday on the level of personality. If we are not careful we can stay on that level. If someone has a pleasing personality we like him. If not, we may tend to avoid him. There does not seem to be any faith in this approach. We are simply going on our likes or dislikes. In a faith community, we are continually called upon to transcend ourselves, to go beyond our natural likings and embrace everyone in the community. This calls for a major form of self-denial. This does not mean we cannot have special friends, but it does mean we have to be friends with every one of our brothers. We cannot be friends with some and indifferent or hostile to others. We are called "brothers" for a reason. We are not blood brothers but something even stronger. We are brothers in Christ; we are brothers in the Spirit. "How pleasant it is when brothers live in unity," says Psalm 131. One of the roles or missions of the Holy Spirit is unity. The locus or the place where this happens in the Church and in our community is the Eucharist. Every other form of community building flows from the Eucharist. These include community dialogues, community work, all aspects of the common life, the way we interact with each other, the way we respect and care for each other, the way we give in to each other, the reverence we show to each other, and the many other ways we exercise mutual service in the community. All of this has its source in the Eucharist.

In a talk about St. Bernard, Emero Stiegman, a Bernardine scholar, beautifully emphasized this notion of community love that flows from the Eucharist. He pointed out that Christ's death on the cross was not an isolated incident in his life. It was the final act of a whole life of sacrifice and giving. We can say the same about the daily celebration of the Eucharist because it informs or graces our whole day, not only in our praise and adoration of the Father, but also in our dealings with each other. The invocation of the Holy Spirit after the consecration at Mass asks that through the power of the Holy Spirit, we may all become one Body, one Spirit in Christ. This is an ongoing grace of the Holy Spirit, an ongoing work of God in our community life. We can never say yes, we are a community now, so we can relax and slow down our effort. While forming community is not entirely up to us, it cannot take place without us. It is one of our missions as cenobites. In a conference to our community on ecclesiology, Susan Wood, SCL, who at the time was a professor of theology at St. John's University in Collegeville, outlined some characteristics of the parish community that I found helpful. She mentioned the universal Church with the pope, the particular Church with the bishop, and the parish Church with the pastor. She then spoke about specialized groups, such as the religious orders. We fall under this category. We are not a parish, but we are still an ecclesial community, the Church of New Melleray. Some of the characteristics of these smaller groups are: (1) Christian in formation, (2) recognized diversity, (3) broad participation—as in community life, (4) connected with the larger Church, and (5) oriented toward mission rather than self-maintenance.

We have to take special effort to keep the last two alive because it is easy for us to feel as though we are not part of the larger Church. It takes constant effort on our part to stay informed about what our diocese is doing and to stay up to date on the teachings of the universal Church. It is also a temptation to move into the realm of self-maintenance, forgetting that we too have a mission in the Church. The Opus Dei (Work of God, or Divine Office) is one of our main duties because it is the prayer of the whole Church. It is the prayer of Jesus to the Father, and we share in his prayer for the good of all. We do not attend the Office for ourselves. All the discipline it takes to be there, to be attentive and reverent, to participate day after day, calls for sacrifice and generosity. This is our way of displacing our self-will and putting mission first.

Another part of our mission is community life. This also takes constant effort and cooperation with the grace of God. Living in a community requires consideration and respect of the other in the promotion of the common good, where the Lord makes his will clearly known.

A further aspect of our mission is prayer in solitude, the silence of our life, the contemplation of God. Praying alone with Jesus is as important as praying his prayer in the Office.

These three forms of mission—liturgical prayer, silent prayer, and the common life—will draw out of us all the self-sacrifice, all the penance and austerity we are capable of offering. We used to characterize our life as a life of penance. It is, but it is not isolated penance. We have all lived with monks who could be called austere and observant but whose efforts seemed to be misplaced or disconnected from our mission in the Church. There is a danger in our type of life to live at a level of self-maintenance, even while living in an austere and observant way.

We are members of a community; we move together, we pray together, and there is real intimacy here.

Gospel Lessons on Brotherly Love[29]

It is interesting how the Gospel lessons of the first week of Lent deal with brotherly love. Here is what a cursory survey of the readings shows us. On Monday, the text is from Matthew 25, where Jesus says, "Whatsoever you do to the least of these brothers you did to me" (Matt 25:40). On Tuesday, there is a passage on forgiveness: "If you forgive others their failings, your heavenly Father will forgive you" (Matt 6:14). The preaching of Jonah is proclaimed on Wednesday. On Thursday, the word is: "Treat others as you would like them to treat you" (Matt 7:12). Then on Friday, the need for reconciliation before offering of a gift is mentioned: "If you are bringing your gifts to the altar and there remember your brother has something against you, leave your offering there before the altar and go and be reconciled with your brother first and then present your offering" (Matt 5:23). Finally, on Saturday, the message centers on love of enemies: "I say to you, love your enemies and pray for those who persecute you" (Matt 5:44).

29. Taken from the chapter talk of March 16, 2003, the Second Sunday of Lent.

In all these readings, we are given a powerful lesson about how to live in community: we should live in a spirit of forgiveness, reconciliation, love of enemies and service. It is a life that calls us to personal repentance and conversion.

To live up to the challenge of the Gospel is not easy. Our natural inclinations draw us in another direction. We are apt to be territorial rather than giving, to claim what is ours rather than to love those who offend us, to react in anger rather than respond with forgiveness, to accentuate others' failings rather than overlook them, to put ourselves first rather than second. We are inclined to isolation rather than reconciliation.

The Gospel teaching, however, focuses on the narrow way that looks to life. It is the great renunciation called for by the cenobitic life. Living this teaching can also be considered part of the monastic vow of obedience. We obey the Gospel teaching by trying to put into practice the words we hear proclaimed in the liturgy, which is a great school of formation. St. Anthony of Egypt received his vocation to be a monk while listening to the word proclaimed in the liturgy. By hearing the Gospel word, we learn how we are to live with each other in community.

Together with the Gospel readings, the lessons from Church documents and spiritual writers also help clarify the meaning of our discipleship. Two significant readings come to mind. One is a passage from a Vatican II document, the Dogmatic Constitution on the Church in the Modern World (or *Gaudium et Spes*). The other is an excerpt from the writings of St. Aelred, a Cistercian Father.

Gaudium et Spes is a sweeping overview of human greatness and weakness. The following excerpt is appropriate for our present world situation:

> The tensions disturbing the world of today are in fact related to a more fundamental tension rooted in the human heart. In the person, many elements are in conflict with each other. On the one side, he has experience of his many limitations as a creature. On the other, he knows there is no limit to his aspirations and that he is called to a higher kind of life.

Then the document goes on to speak of the choices we are compelled to make, observing that

> . . . in our weakness and sinfulness we often do what we do not want to do and fail to do what we would like to do. In consequence we suffer from a conflict within ourselves and this in turn gives rise to so many great tensions in society.[30]

This reminds me of a saying attributed to St. Anthony: "*who sits in solitude and is quiet has escaped three wars: hearing, speaking and seeing. Yet against one thing shall he continuously battle, that is his own heart.*" We can be in solitude and be very silent, but the battle in our own heart continues, and no one is exempt from it. Lent begins in the desert, the symbolic place where we confront and experience the tension in our hearts. Whenever we find ourselves in the midst of a tension that can escalate into a battle or war, the Church reminds us of its source. The council document says it well: "The tensions disturbing the world of today are in fact related to a more fundamental tension rooted in the human heart." There is a temptation to project the inner battle out onto society or the government or the brother next to me. But the real battle is within.

One of the foundational teachings of monastic spirituality is that we must not run from this engagement with our hearts but that we enter the desert and locate the source of conflict right within ourselves. It is equally important that we realize we are not alone in this battle. Christ has gone before us and is with us in our striving. St. Benedict calls the engagement or the interior battle "obedience." Right in the opening lines of the prologue, he says it is the labor of obedience that brings us to Christ, and it is through the continuation of his obedience to the Father that we live. We have two options to choose from in this battle or this tension in our hearts. We can either listen to the promptings of our sinful nature, or we can embrace the cross and listen to the

---

30. The Church in the Modern World, nos. 9–10.

instruction of another voice outside ourselves: *"A voice I did not know said to me, 'Listen carefully, my son, to the precepts of the master.'"* Our vow of obedience is built upon the significance of this interior listening. Incline the ear of your heart.

In the reading from St. Aelred, we find the antidote to the poison that infects our hearts because of our sinful nature. He says:

> If someone wishes to love himself he must not allow himself to be corrupted by indulging his sinful nature. If he wishes to resist the promptings of his sinful nature he must enlarge the whole horizon of his love to contemplate the loving gentleness of the humanity of the Lord. Further, if he wishes to savor the joy of brotherly love with greater perfection and delight he must extend even to his enemies the embrace of true love.[31]

So by expanding our horizons, by opening our hearts even to our enemies, we find true joy in this life. But the key to all this is devotion to Christ Jesus who showed us the way to forgive and love even our enemies.

Aelred goes on to say that "if he wishes to prevent the fire of divine love from growing cold because of injuries received, let him keep the eyes of his soul always fixed on the serene patience of his beloved Lord and Savior."[32] Our Cistercian Fathers had great devotion to the humanity of Christ in his life on earth. As St. Aelred has said: "Your life on earth draws me as the perfume of the beloved attracts the lover."[33]

I began this reflection with several passages from the Gospels on forgiveness and love. Jesus lived each of these teachings. His life on earth is our pole star. He is the way, the truth, and the life for us. It is by following his teachings that we live out our

31. St. Aelred of Rievaulx, *Mirror of Charity*, taken from the Liturgy of the Hours, Friday of the First Week of Lent.

32. St. Aelred of Rievaulx, *Mirror of Charity*, book 3, no. 5 (Kalamazoo, MI: Cistercian Publications, 1990).

33. Op. cit. I, 16.

vow of obedience, the obedience "that will bring us back to him from whom we had drifted through sloth of disobedience" (RB, Prol.).

St. Benedict's Gift: Teaching on Friendship

St. Benedict's Rule for monks is called a classic of Western spirituality. A classic is a work of art, a creative message that speaks to every age; its wealth is never exhausted.

If you look at our Cistercian Fathers, they produced something new based on the Rule of St. Benedict, even though the Rule had been in existence for over six hundred years by their time. You might say what was new, and yet hidden, in the Rule was their teaching on friendship. Nowhere in the Rule will you read that the monks should be friends with each other.

The seed is there, and it waited for the Cistercian renewal to bring it to flower. What is the seed? It is highlighted in today's liturgy in both the Scripture readings and prayers, as well as in the Liturgy of the Hours. One of the great themes running through the liturgy today is unity.

The little passage we heard from Paul's letter to the Ephesians is a wonderful summary of this theme from the Rule: "Bear with one another through love, strive to preserve the unity of the spirit through the bond of peace" (Eph 4:2).

There are many places in the Rule where this teaching is emphasized. It is the undercurrent flowing through the whole Rule of life. As such it is the current flowing through our whole monastic day. A monastic day is different from any other day only in that we try to live out the principles of the Rule, bearing each other in love.

When you get a group of people living together with a shared vision of life, in the normal course of time they become friends. This was known in Benedict's day, but it was not emphasized. It was more or less a by-product of monasticism.

In the Middle Ages, the reality of friendship took center stage. Our Fathers' teaching on friendship is part of our charism, our inheritance. Our Fathers gave a new definition to the monastery: they called it "a school of love." This is a classic statement; it will never be exhausted and it fits all occasions. Love and friendship is the air we breathe.

Perhaps this is a gift monasticism can offer our modern world: an ordered friendship, an ordered love. This friendship is not based on physical attraction or material goods. It is based on a shared vision of what life is all about. It is based on working together to build up the Body of Christ through virtuous living and prayer. It is based on giving up your own will for the sake of the common good. There is thought of personal return, but it is not the primary good that is sought.

St. Benedict did not create monastic life. His generous gift to the Church was to make it accessible to the ordinary Christians. His work is like a vine with many clusters of grapes. All kinds of people, monastic and non-monastic, can enjoy his wine. When people live his rule honestly and thoughtfully, they become friends. They do not set out to become friends. That is not the purpose of the Rule. However, in the process of living the Gospel, people become friends.

This is a great gift St. Benedict gives us.

Friendships in the Monastic Life

At the General Chapter held in Assisi in October 2005, the Abbot General, Dom Bernardo Olivera, spoke of "The Anthropology of Desire at the Service of Monastic Formation." In his conference, he shared that the departure of six or seven young monks during the previous two years had made him reflect on the subject. These were solemnly professed monks. He said that in almost every case there were two common factors: (1) the discovery of human love embodied in a particular woman, and (2) the total relativity given to everything the monk had previously lived.

During the question period after his conference, someone asked for more details on this issue. He said that we should be questioning what kind of formation we are giving in our monasteries. He sees the possible unreality of the monastic life of men in formation. And so he further asked the questions about their formation: (1) What human foundation was the spiritual skyscraper built on? (2) What type of anthropology was implied in the formation process? (3) Are we fostering split personalities, even though we say the opposite? (4) Do we give priority to the spirit in detriment to the body?

These are good questions to reflect on for anyone living the monastic life. It seems to me that one of the main reasons someone would leave to get married after solemn vows is loneliness and lack of intimacy. Someone comes along when a young monk is vulnerable and sweeps him off his feet.

This is unfortunate because friendship and charity are part of our Cistercian inheritance. Our affective needs should be met within the community. Some of the characteristics of an intimate friendship are:

1. Someone you can share anything with.
2. Someone you are not ashamed to tell your secrets to.
3. Someone who becomes one of the centers of your life. If you hear some news, you cannot wait to meet your friend and discuss it.
4. Someone who evokes your affection and love.
5. If a friend dies, you walk around for months saying, I cannot wait to tell him, only to realize he is gone. Friends live in your mind for years.

We can legitimately ask, is this allowed in the monastery? Listen to St. Aelred:

> It is such a great joy to have the consolation of someone's affections—someone to whom you are deeply united by the bonds of love; someone in whom your sprit may find rest; and to whom we may pour out our souls . . . someone to whom we may confide all our thoughts; someone who will weep with you in anxiety, rejoice with you in prosperity, seek with you in doubts; someone you can let into the secret chamber of your mind by the bonds of love, so that even

when absent in body, he is present in spirit. . . . In this life on earth we can love a few people in this way, with heart and mind together, for they are bound to us by the ties of love more than any other."[34]

I do not know if any of us has a friend like this—but even if we have someone we can confide in, we have a great blessing.

What our Cistercian Fathers were teaching is that the dynamics of friendship lead us into the dynamics of love of God. If you have a friendship like St. Aelred describes, you can say you almost lose yourself in the other person. But we can never do that completely, not even in marriage. We can find ourselves in such a relationship but we still stay ourselves; who we are can never be lost.

When it comes to our relationship with Christ, however, we can make that statement. In fact, Paul did. He said, "I live, now not I, but Christ lives in me" (Gal 2:20).

Differentiation is important for maturity but so is union with another. This is the struggle in all human relationships. We cannot give up our individuality, and yet we yearn for union. What we really yearn for is a condition whereby the contrast between differentiation and union is transcended: "a condition in which the affirmation of our individuality is not bought at the price of the denial of union." [35]

Speaking of this type of union, with Christ, St. John of the Cross says, "in the transformation of love each gives possession of self to the other, and each leaves and exchanges self for the other; thus, each one lives in the other and is the other, and both are one in the transformation of love."[36]

Our Fathers spoke of a "ladder of love" (*scala amoris*), where each rung of the ladder is important because it has to do with

---

34. Op. cit., no. 35.

35. Denys Turner, *Eros and Allegory*, Cistercian Studies, no.156 (Kalamazoo, MI: Cistercian Publications, 1995), 58.

36. St. John of the Cross, "The Spiritual Canticle, 12:7," *The Collected Works of St. John of the Cross*, trans. Kieran Kavanaugh, OCD, and Otilio Rodriguez, ocd (Washington, DC: ICS Pubications, 1973).

love. St. Aelred used the image of Noah's ark; he said we should make of our heart a spiritual Noah's ark in which everyone has a place, a share in our love. The basics of this love are all the same, a giving of self to the other, even if this means as little as praying for our enemies. Throughout our life a transformation of all these types of love takes place until we can say, "I live, now not I, but Christ lives in me" (Gal 2:20).

This is what the organization of the monastery is all about. It is a school of love. It was called a *specialis caritatis schola*, a special school of charity, where charity is studied, its problems discussed, and their solution determined.[37]

As our Constitutions say, "The organization of the monastery is directed to bringing the monks into close union with Christ, since it is only through the experience of personal love of the Lord Jesus that the specific gifts of the Cistercian vocation can flower" (Cst. 3:5).

Status Quo Evolving[38]

Today marks the first day of my twentieth year as abbot. As I reflect on the life of our community, I can honestly say we are fortunate enough to have everything we need to live a good monastic life. I am not saying we are not in a fragile situation. With eighty percent of the community over sixty, we certainly are somewhat fragile. When I say we are in a good place, I am talking more about things that are under our control. The spirit in the community is better now than any other time since I have been abbot. We are a mature group of men trying to live the monastic life as best we can.

There is a good climate in the community, a good atmosphere for peacefully living the monastic life. At the same time, we should watch out for complacency or for just coasting along

37. Etienne Gilson, *The Mystical Theology of St. Bernard,* Cistercian Studies, no. 120 (Kalamazoo, MI: Cistercian Publications, 1990), 67.

38. Chapter talk given on January 19, 2003, which marked the twentieth year of my service as abbot of New Melleray.

and letting the status quo become the norm. There is a phrase that was used during the recent General Chapter that describes a desire to change without changing too much. When you do not want to sound like you are against change, or to appear stagnant, you speak of your preference for the "status quo evolving." I think the "status quo evolving" is where we should be. Depending on your outlook, you can emphasize either pole of the phrase, the status quo side or the evolving side.

The change in our life should grow out of who we are rather than coming at us as a radical shift that leaves us asking *"who are we?"* Life is always evolving. Just look back thirty years at New Melleray, and then take a look at where we are today. There have been tremendous changes. Some of them were planned and well thought out. Others just happened.

One of the topics that came up at a recent council meeting was the date of our next community meeting. There was not a lot of enthusiasm, even though one of the visitation recommendations was to have these meetings four times a year. Dom Eamon Fitzgerald (our Father Immediate from Mt. Melleray, Ireland) pointed out that in the past, we might have been a little unrealistic in our approach to community discussions. He mentioned that it is normal for an older group not to want a lot of dialogues. So to have dialogues four times a year seems doable and realistic. I thought it was a good recommendation, very reasonable, something we could easily do. But even this seemed to meet with some resistance, and I must admit it discouraged me. When I read over chapter 3 of the Rule just to refresh myself about what Benedict says, it dawned on me why I was upset.

In chapter 3, we read that the abbot is to call the community together in order to hear what the brothers are thinking. Without this input, he would be acting in a vacuum. The abbot needs the advice of the whole community, not just the council. Community dialogues and open forum discussions are vital sources of knowledge for the abbot, because they enable him to learn what is on people's minds. It gives him a sense of their emotional life, of their intellectual life, and of their monastic feel for things. It really is a vital link for anyone having to make decisions and give leadership to the community.

It will also be helpful to hear your thoughts about the issue of inculturation. We are assimilating new people into the community, asking them to change and become like us. This is nearly a total adaptation on their part, all the way from the clothes they wear to the times to go to bed at night and get up in the morning. Their whole day is planned hour by hour. There is indeed a tremendous change taking place in a postulant's or a novice's lifestyle. Moreover, we should be more aware of how every new entry changes us in ever so subtle ways as we adapt to each person's personality. We have to ask ourselves how well we are doing in introducing new people into our way of life. Do we make them feel welcome? Do we pass on the monastic tradition to them? What kind of cultural realities exist that might not have existed several years ago? We must remember that formation is not a one-way street. Our community has to adapt in order to assimilate. Candidates are generally older these days, and this means they have had more life experiences than many of us had when we entered. A good example would be the professional and work backgrounds they bring with them. We cannot just ignore that and expect a forty-year-old man to act like a nineteen-year-old teenager.

The evolving part of the status quo is our challenge.

THANKSGIVING DAY REFLECTIONS

Thanksgiving as a Faith Event

We probably all have various images of Thanksgiving Day, ranging from the famous scene of the pilgrims and Indians dining on roast turkey to our own family holiday celebrations. These images convey harmony and peace, friendship and fellowship, in order to remind us that in working together we can make America better.

Some of the words found in Scripture can better clarify the cultural concept of fellowship. One such word is *koinonia*, which is found in St. Paul's first letter to the Corinthians (1:9). It is a

Greek word meaning community, fellowship, or partnership. It is what the picture on so many Thanksgiving Day cards is meant to convey: a community and a fellowship between diverse people. It is what makes us travel great distances to be home for Thanksgiving because we all have a deep desire for community, and everyone wants to participate in some form of partnership. It is what drives people to get married, to join religious communities, even paradoxically, to become hermits.

Hermits and contemplative communities can speak eloquently about *koinonia* because they point to the source of this archetypal need for togetherness. It is a profound need, a deep desire in the human heart because it comes from God. God is the source of our heart's desire for union, and this is what breaks down the borders that separate people.

In the Gospel stories, Jesus constantly cuts through the borders that keep us from finding our true heart's desire. In Luke 17:11-19, we see Jesus walking on the border between Samaria and Galilee. This border is symbolic, and unfortunately it is still very real. It is a border that separates and divides. Luke tells us that Jesus encounters a group of Samaritan lepers whom he heals and sends on their way. Only one returns—someone who has crossed many borders and been an outcast, an unclean and leprous Samaritan, who in the course of the story finds his heart's desire, his true being, the all-important other in his life. He speaks out of that experience. Luke even says he shouts at the top of his voice giving praise and thanks to God. This nobody has crossed life's most difficult border from disbelief to belief. It is a border we all must confront. Can we not see ourselves in this Gospel? At least today, let us be the one who returns and gives thanks to God for making us cut through the borders we ourselves have created, and let us be one with him and one another.

Constant Gratefulness to God

In one of the many discussions we have had about the renovation of our infirmary, we talked about the layout of rooms, the types of fixtures, the colors of the walls, and numerous other details, and I have been reminded of the two years from 1974 to 1976, when we were renovating the church. We had so many decisions to make, and since we were talking about construction, the decisions were final—they were etched in stone! One decision we faced with the church had to do with its stone walls. At the time the original church was built, the stones were never meant to be exposed. From 1871 to 1974 they were hidden behind thick plaster. So when we took the plaster off we had to clean and tuck-point the stone. Frank Kacmarcik, our design consultant, told us to treat the walls as you would an old barn and to smear the plaster on instead of making each joint distinct. The idea was to pull the wall together visually. This suggestion scared us, because there was no going back once the decision was made. But Frank proved right; the huge stone walls of this church pull together in a unity. When I am distracted in choir sometimes I look at the stones in the wall. There is a pleasing regular irregularity about them. They are not uniform in shape. They are very different in fact, and yet there is a unity there. The analogy, of course, is with our community, or for that matter, with a family. The individual members are so different and yet they are all one community, one family. Togetherness does not come easily for Americans. We prize the rugged individual, the autonomous self.

Abraham Lincoln was the president who called for the first national celebration of a Day of Thanksgiving. It was an attempt to pull together a nation torn apart by war. I suppose we could be cynical and say the attempt has failed, but on the whole I think our nation celebrates Thanksgiving Day with due reverence. Even here in the monastery, Thanksgiving Day is a day to stop and reflect on the role gratitude plays in our life, especially since today's Gospel reminds us how rare gratitude is: "It seems," Jesus says, "no one has come back to thank God but this foreigner" (Luke 17:18). Ten lepers were healed, but only one came back to thank the Lord. The other nine were probably so busy enjoying their new life that they did not have time to return with their thanks. The story is meant to make us ask who we are like. Are we like the nine who went on their way, or are we like the one who returned? Are we the nine as a nation, as a community, as individuals? Are we enjoying the bounty, the harvest, of life so much that we forget where it comes from? Or are we like the one who returns to the source of the good?

God stands at the center of our lives just as Jesus stands at the center of the Gospel story. Jesus is the source of the gift of healing, but he is easily forgotten. He does not force himself into the lives of the ten lepers. Only one of them makes the connection between his good fortune and the role Jesus plays in it, and he is the one you would least expect to make it. The story is scary. It teaches us that not only do most people forget who they are but the one who remembers is a foreigner, a nobody, someone we think can teach us nothing. And yet, he is the only one who shines. He is the only one with real insight into life.

God is central to our personal story, but he is easily forgotten. God will not usually overwhelm us. Jesus portrays God as knocking at the door of our lives waiting to enter. He will not come uninvited. The connection between the life we enjoy and God is easily forgotten. Actually the connection we have with our nation, our community, and our families is easily forgotten. We can be individual, discreet stones in a very boring wall, or bonded together by love into something beautiful.

St. Paul gives us a design to pull us together when he says in the second reading today: "You are to be clothed in heartfelt compassion, in generosity and humility, gentleness and patience. Bear with one another, forgive each other. . . . Over all these clothes put on love, the perfect bond. Always be thankful" (Col 3:14).

Christ at the Heart of Unity in Community

I come to this Thanksgiving Day[39] with gratitude in my heart for the community and for the faithfulness that makes it possible for us all to live here. I believe we have a rock-solid community

39. This section is adapted from the chapter talk on November 21, 2004, the Sunday after Thanksgiving Day. It coincided with the Solemnity of Christ the King, the closing Sunday of the Church's liturgical year.

life. It is a community we can trust to be faithful to the Cistercian life, with each one contributing his service to the community. I am not simply referring to the work side of this service but also to what each one brings of himself to the Liturgy of the Hours, to meals, and to all the aspects of the common life. In the midst of all these, each one is bearing each other's burdens: the strong helping the weak, mercy prevailing over sacrifice. That harmonious living together is the vision of St. Benedict's Rule. The balance of the life is the Cistercian charism for our times.

Our community is blessed in so many ways. We know what we are about. We have learned to accept each other and respect each other. Of course, every community can improve. Any improvements we may work on, however, come from a good foundation. We have good attendance in choir. We help one another in resolving interpersonal conflicts. We may recall that there were times in our history when conflict resolution might have been necessary, but right now we are enjoying peace and it is something to be thankful for.

But whence this peace? Is it a real peace or just a tired sigh of "peace at all cost"? I think it is a real peace for the following reasons.

Ours is a peace that comes from within. When the majority of the community has a strong interior life, a place that is rock solid, then we are not blown about from one place to another. We are not changing course all the time. We have been through enough changes that we have had to establish ourselves as a sure foundation or else perish. In today's reading at Vigils, we heard St. Bernard speak about a harmony of wills. He said that God is present in all creatures, but only the rational ones can embrace him by knowledge, and only the good ones by love. This love is a harmony of wills, God's will and our will united. Love leads to the deepest knowledge. It is only when you love someone that you really know him. Knowledge that comes from love is the best type of knowledge. It is to know God as we are known by God; it is total likeness. This comes about in prayer. It follows that a mature, solid community, a community where chaos is at a minimum, is a community that prays. Each one is involved in interior prayer, in harmony with the will of God. This is a community that can provide a secure place for the formation of new vocations.

The other aspect to our unity is each individual's love of Christ. This unites us like nothing else can. In his book *The Splendor of the Church*, Cardinal Henri de Lubac[40] explains this love of Christ. He begins by saying that it is hard to imagine people more remote from us than the Alexandrians of the third century or the Africans of the fourth century. Their issues and problems are not ours, and for this reason, it can be difficult to relate to what was written at the time. Reading the Fathers of the Church can be tedious, but then at the turn of a page, there is the name of Christ, and everything comes to life again: "We become aware of fine shades of response which parallel our own for us, down to the subtlest nuances." In Christ, Origen and Augustine are our contemporaries, our fathers and our brothers. We become, in Augustine's words, "a group of reasonable beings united among themselves by a love having the same object."

This is what unites our community and makes it so strong. We share the same love, and it is the Lord Jesus who is the same object of that love. We all look in the same direction because we have one and the same Lord.

All of us who have made solemn vows have been called to live here together, each one centered on the love of Christ, each one united in that love. We welcome others who are discerning that call. Being given a Cistercian vocation is a wonderful grace. It is not something we do totally on our own. It is a call, an interior impulse to love the Lord Jesus in this Cistercian monastery. Without this center of love in the heart, the vocation can die. With this strong center, not only can we survive anything, but we also can overcome anything, even death itself.

This is why I think that we have a good community, one where chaos does not rule, where the predictable has not broken

40. Henri de Lubac, *The Splendor of the Church*, trans. Michael Mason (New York: Sheed and Ward, 1956), 32–34.

down. I am not saying that we do not have areas that need improving. Communications can always be improved, so can the observances and the participation in community activities, but as long as we possess the one thing necessary, we have the essential ingredient of a Cistercian, contemplative community. It is a great blessing and something for which we are thankful.

Chapter Four

TREASURES OF MONASTIC VALUES

Origen once said that no one can understand the Gospel of John unless he has received Mary as his mother and laid his head on Jesus' breast. In other words, it is not through scholarly research alone that we come to knowledge of the Gospels. It is through intimacy with the persons of Jesus and Mary. It is through a personal relationship with the two key figures of the Gospels.

We might say something similar about the monastic life. It is not through study that we know it. It is through love. By love I mean the awakening of the heart. If you do not live in a monastery, then reading about monastic spirituality may be all that is available to you. How, then, can your monastic heart awaken? It happens when deep calls to deep, as the psalmist says: when the deep of your heart is touched by the word that is monastic spirituality. Is there one word that can sum this up? Not really, but if there were, it would be the word *heart*. The heart is the deepest core of our being. It is the center, a spiritual place where our life and God's life meet. A monk is meant to live in this place all the time because it is the place of continual prayer.

The chapter talks that follow are an attempt to speak of this place. If you find your heart responding, awakening, longing, desiring God—then know that in its depths, your soul is finding its true home.

SILENCE, SOLITUDE, AND ENCLOSURE

The Monastic Value of Silence

On the occasion of the community's annual retreat,[41] it is good to practice more silence than usual. Our Constitution 24 states that "silence is counted among the principal monastic values of the Cistercian Order." In times of monastic decline, the two values that were neglected were poverty and silence. The Constitutions note that silence does six things:

1. It assures solitude for the monk in the community.
2. It fosters mindfulness of God.
3. It fosters fraternal communion.
4. It opens the mind to the aspiration of the Holy Spirit.
5. It favors attentiveness of the heart.
6. It favors solitary prayer to God.

So silence assures solitude for the monk in the community, and it fosters fraternal communion. That might sound like a contradiction because society is so accustomed to thinking that the best way to foster communion is by doing a lot of talking. While it is true that communication requires spoken dialogue, here in the monastery we also foster fraternal communion by being silent even when we are together. This assures the necessary solitude for prayer.

At New Melleray, we have a community guideline that states: ". . . out of the awareness of the mystery of our vocation will arise a respect for the vocation and personal solitude of our brothers. Our deepest communion with each other is realized in our communion in silence." That is a pretty powerful statement: "our deepest communion with each other is realized in our communion in silence." This is not something that happens overnight. The

---

41. It is usually around the month of January that the community holds its annual retreat. This talk on silence was given on January 23, 2005, on the eve of the retreat directed by Dom Joseph Delargy of Mt. St. Bernard Abbey, England.

awareness of the mystery of our vocation unfolds slowly, and it is only after many years of monastic living that we realize communication with each other happens through silence. Moreover, our guideline also states that "our responsibility to our brother is to preserve the atmosphere of quiet so that he will be free to enter more deeply into the silence of his own heart." Preserving an atmosphere of quiet is a respectful act of fraternal charity intended to help our brothers attain the prayer of the heart.

During a community retreat we may tend to focus on the conferences that are presented by the retreat director. Sometimes we even go so far as to judge the success of the retreat by the quality of the conferences. But there is a deeper element to consider. Our annual retreat is an opportune time to examine ourselves with regard to our practice of silence and its importance in our life. We no longer have the many rules and regulations that helped us, almost forced us, to practice silence in the past. Now it is left to us to live out of a deep conviction that an atmosphere of silence is essential to our monastic life. Coming from the culture in which we grew up, our first impulse is to speak and to communicate by talking. It is a difficult learning curve to communicate by silence.

Our Constitutions conclude by listing three other values of silence. It fosters mindfulness of God. It opens the mind to the inspiration of the Holy Spirit. It favors attentiveness of heart and solitary prayer to God. There is almost a causal sequence in these statements. Attentiveness of heart leads to mindfulness of God. Mindfulness of God opens the mind to the inspiration of the Holy Spirit, which brings us into solitary prayer to God. Solitary prayer to God is the blossom, the fruit that is nourished in the soil of silence.

Paradise of Solitude

We all know what it is like to lose our concentration during the liturgy. One of the worst times for me is during the concluding orations at the end of Lauds and Vespers. My mind wanders, my hearing is not what it used to be, and I must admit, sometimes the hebdomadary mumbles. All this combines to leave a blank space in my head where the closing prayer should be!

However, last Tuesday at Vespers, a phrase from the closing prayer caught my attention. It pertained to "confessing our sin without blaming others." I walked out of Vespers saying to myself, "I hope so and so hears that!" I couldn't help thinking how easy it is to blame others when we fail or sin. There used to be a stand-up comic on TV in the 50s whose signature phrase was, "The devil made me do it." The devil can tempt us, but he can never force us to sin.

A few days later, I went back and reread the entire prayer, which was taken from a book compiled by the French liturgy commission and translated by Fr. Nivard Kinsella of Roscrea, one of our Cistercian houses in Ireland. The prayer seemed totally new to me even though we had been saying it every two weeks for a long time. It goes like this: "Lord, as you once walked in the garden in the calm of evening, you come and seek us. If we flee from your presence, change our fear to confidence. Confessing our sin without blaming others, we place our hope in your mercy and forgiveness."

This prayer contains two major monastic themes. The first is the garden of paradise. The second is recognizing our sin instead of judging others. I want to comment on the first part of the prayer and focus on the garden.

From the very beginning and all throughout the Middle Ages, monks have looked upon their cloister as the garden of paradise, a place of peace, tranquility, repose, and contemplation. In many of our Cistercian monasteries the Latin words *Pax Huic Intrantibus* were engraved above the porter's lodge or entrance: "Peace to all who enter here."

Our Cistercian Fathers constructed their monasteries in remote places, "away from the haunts of men." Many early monasteries were built in valleys rather than on mountaintops for the purpose of ensuring silence and solitude. The valleys were quiet. Mountaintops were too visible, there was too much to excite the eye and distract the mind. The valley bespeaks calm and still-ness—from the Latin *quies*, for quiet and peace. In fact, the motto of New Melleray is *Vacate et Videte*, from Psalm 45:9 (46:9), trans-lated as "Be Still and Know" or "Be Empty and See."

In an ideal monastic climate or atmosphere, everything should lead to this interior stillness of mind. Be still, be empty and see. Keeping our minds still is a monastic discipline. Keeping our lives empty does not mean sterility. There is fullness in mo-nastic emptiness.

John Cassian says that those who are full jeer at the honey-comb! In other words, when you are full, you even turn away from delicious food. He said this after his long discourse on the words, "O God, come to my assistance, O Lord, make haste to help me." He encouraged monks to make this phrase a continual prayer because it can be used all day long, in every situation, whether standing or sitting or walking or remaining still. No matter what a monk may be doing he can keep the words "God, come to my assistance, O Lord, make haste to help me" on his lips. Cassian also wrote about the "poverty of this prayer" in terms of keeping our lives lean. Instead of filling our minds with all kinds of distract-ing thoughts, we are supposed to be mindful of God.

In 1963 Dom Jean Leclercq published a study on the con-templative vocabulary of the monastic Middle Ages, including words like Sabbath, *otia* (idleness), *quies, vacatio,* and many others that represent the contemplative side of our monastic life. It is a side that can easily be lost in a big monastery with a lot of neces-sary work to keep it going.

We have to make sure we have time for contemplative prayer, for *lectio,* and for study. All these practices call for interior stillness, a certain level of tranquility, a climate of silence and recollection. There are times when our vocation calls us to be alone, to live in solitude. Sometimes it is only after years of faith-ful practice that this side of our life reveals its sweetness.

Orthodox monasticism places a greater emphasis on the quiet side of monastic life than we do in the West. Two words figure prominently in the Eastern Orthodox monastic spirituality, namely, *hesychia* and *apatheia*. *Hesychia* is rest in God. *Apatheia* literally means passionlessness, but I have seen it compared to Cassian's teaching on purity of heart. It refers to that calm that results from integrating all our drives and passions so that we can focus on the central mystery of God living in us and we in God.

There is another Greek word, *nepsis*, meaning sobriety of thoughts, which we translate as "guard of the heart." We close the door of our hearts to everything that pulls us out of our recollection, everything that stirs up our anger or passions. If we stop temptations in their infancy when they are only thoughts, they will never give birth to actions.

These practices are meant to free us for the one thing necessary. Here in the monastery we have everything we need, and the interior atmosphere is one of peace. Let the abbot arrange things so no one is troubled in the house of God, exhorts St. Benedict.

Compared to other ways of life, we are on a vacation, a vacation, that is, free from the many obligations of those in the clergy and the active religious orders. But this freedom brings with it its own obligations. We have to be deeply immersed in our contemplative life. We have to take its practices seriously to justify the freedom from responsibilities which the Church has given us. This is more evident to me now than it was fifty years ago. With such a shortage of priests, how can we justify having priests among us who are part of our monastic community and are not involved with parish responsibilities? We cannot, unless we are serious about our vocation.

Another theme connected with the garden of paradise is the angelic life. It is said the angels live in the "presence of God." Similarly then, the monk is someone who lives the angelic life insofar as his main occupation is to adore and praise God: "To stand in his presence and serve you."

The monastic liturgy has been portrayed as a mirror image of the angelic liturgy of heaven. This idea is very strong in the Divine Liturgy of the Orthodox tradition. We in the West still have the Hymn of the Angels on feast days and the Holy, Holy, Holy everyday. There is an eschatological element to all this. Monks anticipate the end time. They are occupied now with eternal values. Our prayer of praise and adoration anticipates the heavenly choirs of angels.

It is so easy to lose the contemplative side of our life. It can be swallowed up by the busyness each day brings. This can just be a subtle form of *acedia*—that boredom or dullness of soul that kills the whole contemplative dimension of our life. It is very hard to practice recollection and silence when the reality behind the practice seems absent. We can easily become bored. But if we remain faithful to our practice, we will someday enjoy the fruits of our labor. St. Aelred speaks of the six days of toil that come before the one day of Sabbath rest.

In chapter 19 of the Rule, entitled "The Discipline of Psalmody," St. Benedict reminds us to behave in choir as if we were in the presence of God and his angels (RB 19:6). The Latin phrase is *in conspectu divinitatis*. If we live in this way, even though we do not experience the Divine Presence, someday God will reveal himself to his faithful servants. Then our hearts will be enlarged and we will run in the way of the Lord with "unspeakable sweetness of Love" (RB Prol. 49).

On Solitude and Enclosure

In Constitution 29 of the 1990 edition of the Constitutions of our Order, enclosure was called "separation from the world." In the 2005 General Chapter we voted to change the heading to "Solitude and Monastic Enclosure."

The opening sentence gives a very brief spirituality of enclosure. It begins with the words, "The monastery is a place of solitude and communion." That phrase underscores the importance of finding a balance between time spent alone and time spent in community.

What I have found in my own life and from observing others is that individuals are drawn to one or more of the essential

dimensions of our life. A person might, by grace and temperament, be drawn to solitude, someone else to *lectio*, another to
manual labor or the Office or interior prayer and meditation. This
diversity is one of the beauties of our monastic vocation. The
monastery is a garden with many flowers. Someone is attracted
to a particular flower and someone else to another. But the garden
is enclosed; it is something like a world within the world. Everything we do in our garden is for the beauty of the world. We do
not live for ourselves. We live to build up the whole Body of
Christ, for the good of the entire world.

The text continues: "The monastery is a place of solitude
and communion where those who prefer nothing to the love of
Christ seek the face of God, and so make themselves strangers
to the ways of the world, giving themselves to a more intense
prayer, thus taking part in the solitary prayer of Jesus for the
entire world."

Two of the phrases in that passage come to us from the Rule
of St. Benedict. They are "to prefer nothing to the love of Christ"
and "to make themselves a stranger to the ways of the world"
(RB 4:20). Some wanted this last phrase to be omitted but the
chapter voted to keep it in the text. The last phrase, however, is
new: "taking part in the solitary prayer of Jesus for the entire
world." Personally, I think "sharing" would be a better term than
"taking part," because the idea of sharing in the prayer of Jesus
is very important. It goes right to the heart of our life and to the
true meaning of solitude and enclosure.

The saints are the ones who had insight and experience in
sharing in the life of Jesus. In the last pages of her autobiography,
The Story of a Soul, St. Therese borrows the high priestly prayer
of Jesus as recorded in John 17 and appropriates it. She said she
is bold enough to take his words and make them her own and
give them back to the Father as her own prayer. St. Cyprian reminds us that when we say the Our Father, the Father in heaven
sees his Son praying those words in us. On the feast of St. Pio of
Pietralcina (Padre Pio), we heard him say, "I need to love you
more and more but I do not have any more love in my heart. I

have given all my love to you. If you want more, fill my heart with your love, and then oblige me to love you more and I will not refuse you."[42] For me, this principle of exchange is at the heart of the Jesus Prayer, "Lord Jesus Christ, Son of God, have mercy on me, a sinner." To pray that prayer is almost like breathing. We do not make a decision to take each breath. We just breathe subconsciously. It is the same with this kind of prayer, and when it happens we pass from "strenuous prayer" to "self-acting prayer," from my prayer to the prayer of Christ in me. This is why an Orthodox monk said the most important thing to learn in prayer is silence. "You yourself," he says, "must be silent; let the prayer speak."[43]

The place for this type of prayer is the place of the heart. Formation in the monastic life is formation of the heart. Once we have found our hearts, we move from the effort of prayer, the work of prayer, from strenuous prayer to self-acting prayer. The heart has two meanings. It is the center of our being and the point of meeting between each of us and God. Two do not exist in this place, but only One. Our prayer becomes Christ's prayer. There in the heart we live and move and have our being. I like Thomas Merton's explanation of this: "At the center of our being is a point of nothingness which is untouched by sin and by illusion, a point of pure truth, a point or spark that belongs entirely to God, which is never at our disposal, from which God disposes of our lives, which is inaccessible to the fantasies of our mind or the brutalities of our will. This little point of nothingness and of absolute poverty is the pure glory of God in us. . . . I have no program for this seeing. It is only given. But the gate of heaven is everywhere."[44]

42. St. Pio of Pietrelcina, taken from the Breviary, Office of Readings, September 23.

43. Kallistos Ware, *The Power of the Name* (Oxford: Fairacres Press, 1979), 1.

44. Thomas Merton, *Conjectures of a Guilty Bystander* (Garden City, NY: Doubleday, 1966).

In Assisi, at the 2005 General Chapter, I picked up a little treatise by St. Bonaventure called *The Journey of the Mind into God.*[45] It is his only mystical work, and in it he talks about leaving our outer life and entering into ourselves and seeing God in the mirror of our own souls. He says, "It is here that the light of truth shines like the light of a candelabrum upon the face of our mind in which the image of the Most Blessed Trinity shines in splendor." Then he goes on: ". . . it becomes clear that the soul itself is an image of God and a similitude so present to itself that it actually grasps God and potentially 'has the capacity for God' and the ability to participate in God" (chap. III).

Contemplation for St. Bonaventure unfolds in stages. The first stage is the vestiges, that is, the vestige or imprint of God in everything he created. By our senses, especially our sight, we see all the beauty of creation. A contemplative sees more. He sees the vestige, the impress of the Divine present in this beauty. The second stage is the image within the self, the image of God in each human being. Our human intellects can take us only so far into the self. Faith opens us to our own beauty, our own heart, which is the image of God. Bonaventure says, "Here you can see God through yourself as through an image. And this is to see through a mirror in an obscure manner."[46] The final stage is when, having contemplated creation and the soul, we "pass over and transcend not only the visible world but the soul itself. In this passage Christ is the way and the door. Christ is the ladder and the vehicle."[47] Bonaventure says we rest with Christ in the tomb as one dead to the outer world, yet experiencing, as far as possible in this pilgrim state, what was said on the cross to the thief: "This day you will be with me in Paradise" (Luke 23:43). This is our journey into God.

45. St. Bonaventure, *The Journey of the Mind into God*, Franciscan Institute Publications (New York: St. Bonaventure University, 2002).

46. Ibid., chap. III.

47. Ibid., chap. VII, 2.

Arriving at these stages into God can only be accomplished in solitude, in the enclosure of our hearts. No one can take us there but God. We cannot share this place with anyone but God.

A Cistercian speaking about solitude and enclosure can only express the reality in so many words, but the words are based on centuries of monastic experience. We, the monks of today, are still in the formation process. We have all the teachings of the Fathers, all the words of our monastic tradition and patrimony. We have all the observances of our Cistercian life. We read and live out the tradition every day. What our hearts cry out for is the experience. We want the experience that St. Bernard had, that St. Francis and St. Bonaventure had, and that St. Therese and Padre Pio had. This is our inheritance. We may not have the intensity of the great saints, but if we are faithful and daily give ourselves to prayer and contemplation, slowly and gradually our divine life will be revealed to us and in us.

Hiddenness of the Contemplative Life

We once read a book in the refectory entitled *Walking the Bible*.[48] It was an interesting approach and very different from ours since we are used to approaching the Bible passage on our knees. In fact, we used to have a custom here in the community to begin our *lectio divina* by reading the first few sentences of the Bible on our knees.

The Bible is the Word of God. When Fr. Claude Pieper once spoke to us, he quoted *Dei Verbum*, the Vatican II document on Divine Revelation. He said that when God communicates in the Sacred Scriptures, he is not communicating only in words, but he is also giving himself to us. It is divine revelation. It seems to me that any other approach makes the Bible just another book. The Bible is a very special book, and there is no other one like it. We believe the Holy Spirit is the ultimate author and all the

48. Bruce Feiler. *Walking the Bible: A Journey by Land Through the Five Books of Moses* (New York: Morrow Press, 2001).

Scriptures point to the revelation of Jesus, whose birth in the flesh we celebrate at Christmas.

The book we read in the refectory approaches the Bible in what Cardinal Henri de Lubac calls the error of extrinsicism and historicism. In extrinsicism one moves directly from historical existence to an assertion of faith in such a way that historical evidence becomes demonstrable proof of faith. In other words, if you can prove that the historical events of the Bible are accurate and historically verifiable, say, by archaeology or DNA, or whatever, then you have proof of your faith. This is like basing your faith in the Resurrection on the Shroud of Turin. The problem with all historically based arguments is that if science proves them inaccurate, then you have no grounds for believing. Our faith does not rest on science. It rests on the witness of the apostles. Faith comes through hearing the Word proclaimed in the liturgy. Faith is a gift, not something we can reason to. Faith and reason go hand in hand of course, but faith is not reason. Faith is a supernatural virtue. As the letter to the Hebrews says: "Only faith can guarantee the blessings that we hope for, or prove the existence of realities that are unseen" (11:1). It is for their faith that our ancestors are acknowledged.

Only faith can prove the existence of realities that are unseen. Our whole monastic life is a life of faith. There is an unseen dimension to our life, an invisible dimension, a faith dimension. If our faith becomes weak or lost, then we are just a group of men living together, perhaps enjoying each other's company and bonding together to make life bearable. But we would not be a faith-based community.

Our community is an extension of the Incarnation. It is the life of Jesus made visible. Let me invite you to reflect on some aspects of our community life that we tend to take for granted.

Consider for a moment all the things that are done for us. We are provided with three meals a day, with clothes to wear, with a house to live in that is heated for our comfort, and lighted so we can read. All our medical needs are taken care of and paid for. We have cars available to us. All the books we need are in a large library. Just these few things put us among the most privileged people in the world.

Beyond all these material things we are cared for with love. Our brothers give us respect. Some of our affective needs are met through friendships. We reverence each other. We do all this and more for one another because we represent Christ to each other. How we treat each other is how we treat Christ. The pericope in Matthew 25 is very powerful. Jesus tells us: "Whatsoever you do to the least, you do to me" (Matt 25:40).

Serving each other in community is an act of faith. If we neglect this central duty, strange things can happen. We can receive all the benefits of the community without giving our share. We can take for granted what is provided and eventually become institutionalized. This can easily happen to any of us if we forget why so much is provided for us. The community provides these things so we can live a life of prayer. When one person provides the heat, the rest of us do not have to spend time heating our rooms. When two people cook our meals, the rest of us are spared the time and can concentrate on *lectio*, the Divine Office, prayer, study, silence, and solitude. All this happens to be a great luxury in our society. It is not easy to live a life of penance and self-denial in such circumstances. But if we waste the time given us, then the heart goes out of our life.

We have a role in the Church, a mission. We are set aside for a purpose. We are not expected to respond to the demands of the apostolic life. The bishop cannot ask our priests to take on the responsibilities of a parish even in these difficult times when parishes are closing for lack of priests. We have been granted the role of contemplatives in the Church. With that designation comes the responsibility to live a certain way and that has been outlined for us in the Rule of St. Benedict and in our Constitutions. Thus we also have to follow the way in our hearts through our prayer in community, the Opus Dei, and in solitude.

Our schedule or horarium is set up for prayer, for nothing else but prayer. It is a poor schedule from a business point of view, or even from the perspective of someone in one of the active religious orders. But the monastic schedule has a distinct purpose. It frees us to give our time to prayer.

Our community is blessed with so many monks who are faithful to their vocation. You see them adapting in their own way to changing situations, making hidden sacrifices to be faithful to their life of prayer, to their life of sacrifice, not giving in to the temptation to take the easier way, not compromising their ideals. Such faithfulness is not easy, because the structure is not as inflexible as it was thirty years ago. There is a greater freedom of choice now, a greater adaptation to modern times. It requires a firmer resolve on the part of monks in order not to compromise their personal lives. We see one another working hard to provide for the community, rising early to pray, remaining faithful to the Office day after day, never missing a beat, going about tasks quietly, almost unnoticed, living the hidden life. It is a life similar to the hidden life of Jesus at Nazareth. This is one of the gifts of our monastic way and one of the reasons the contemplative life has always had a special appeal in the life of the Church.

Search for the Hidden God

On the occasion of the feast of St. Benedict (July 11), I would like to speak about some themes that surfaced during today's Scripture readings.

The first reading was from the book of Proverbs. In my New Jerusalem Bible, the book of Proverbs has a prologue that begins: "Listen, my son, to your father's instruction" (Prov 1:8). We are familiar with that text since St. Benedict used it to open the prologue to his Rule and set the tone for what followed. In a sense he was setting the tone for all of our monastic life by presenting it to us in the context of the wisdom tradition of the Sacred Scriptures. Today's reading for the feast of St. Benedict begins: ". . . my son, take my words to heart" (Prov 2:1). It goes on for six verses about knowledge and understanding or clear perception and wisdom.

When I read the text, I realized how important it is in the monastic life to be able to listen. To be able to listen to a voice that is not your own, that is the key. To be able to listen to a voice that is not your own is not as easy as it may seem. We have various slang expressions to describe people who cannot listen. "He lives in his own world," we say, or "You cannot break through to him," or "He is impossible to reach."

We all have areas where this could be said of us, but in general, to be a monk means to be open to the teaching of another. To be able to hear the other—the other is the abbot, the community, your neighbor, the prior, the novice master and a whole host of other voices. Of course, the primary voice is the one that comes from a divine source, from the liturgy, prayer, or *lectio divina*. St. Bernard speaks of the visitation of the Word which comes to us in many ways. A certain mature docility is needed in order to hear it. This is something we must foster all our life.

In footnote 2a of chapter 2 of Proverbs, the New Jerusalem Bible says, "All wisdom comes from God, but the dispositions needed for receiving it are an enquiring mind and a willingness to learn the teachings of one's elders."

An enquiring mind is a focused mind, a searching mind. The object of the search is God. "Are they truly seeking God?" St. Benedict asks of novices. In the monastic tradition an enquiring mind is not the same thing as a curious mind. Curiosity is a distraction. Enquiry and searching have a clear goal and direction. "We are to look for understanding as if for silver, search for it as though for a buried treasure" (Prov 2:4). There should be a certain healthy drive about our monastic life. We are searching for a buried treasure. We are not just standing around waiting for something to happen. Our life has a direction and a passion. Keeping that passion alive requires effort. *Acedia*, a real spiritual illness, sucks the passion out of our life or misdirects it. The two classic expressions of *acedia* are boredom and wanderlust, and we see them in the monk who cannot sit still, who is always into something that distracts from his spiritual quest.

We believe that our life has a hidden fruitfulness for the Church. Hidden means just that. We cannot see it. It is difficult to keep something before our eyes when we cannot see it. We cannot measure the results of our efforts in the monastic life. We cannot say we got so many hundreds of people out of purgatory with our prayers. Our life is a life of faith, a life of prayer. Any growth will come in the form of humility and love, not in numbers and measures. I believe absence plays an important role in our life. There is the absence of results, absence of a sense satisfaction, or even the absence of God.

St. Benedict tells us we live continually in the sight of God, *ab aspectu divinitatis.* We live under the Divine Gaze. God sees us but we do not see him. Our eyes do not look on God, and so we usually experience the absence of God more than his presence. Monks have to get used to this. But this absence can be a beautiful thing. The absence of God is not like the absence of a person. Simone Weil used to say that contact with human beings is given us through the sense of presence; contact with God is given through the sense of absence. She then weighs these two and concludes that the absence of God has more to it than the presence of another person.

This is also the teaching of the great theologians and mystics. St. Thomas Aquinas makes a series of statements about what we do not know about God. He reminds us that God is a spirit and so we must deny him all corporeal things as well as intellectual things, like goodness and wisdom. What remains, then, is only that God exists. Then Aquinas goes on to say we must even remove from God his very existence, as we understand creatures to exist. The result is that our minds remain in the darkness of total ignorance through which we are best united to God in a perfect state of life. Living in the absence of God is not the same as experiencing the emptiness of *acedia,* the boredom of it all! There is a paradoxical fullness in this absence.

Another way of looking at this absence comes from John of the Cross who says, "you should never desire satisfaction in what you understand about God, but in what you do not understand about Him. Never stop with loving and delighting in your understanding and experience of God, but love and delight in what is neither understandable nor perceptible of Him. Such is the way of seeking Him in Faith."[49]

We seek the hidden God. To truly seek him means we seek in faith. God is hidden from our faculties of knowing. Faith takes over where our intellect ends. Love is our guide. Faith and love are the blind man's guide, says St. John of the Cross.[50] We have a temptation to think that the experience of the absence of God means he is far away from us, just because we do not understand, taste, or experience him. But St. John says: "The less distinct is (our) understanding of Him, the closer we approach Him since in the words of the prophet David, He made darkness His hiding place. Thus in drawing near Him, you will experience darkness because of the weakness of your eye."[51]

This is reinforced by a text from *The Cloud of Unknowing*: "Concerning our prayer, you will seem to know nothing and to feel nothing except the naked intent toward God in the depths of your being. Try as you might this darkness and this cloud will remain between you and your God. You will feel frustrated, for your mind will be unable to grasp Him and your heart will not relish the delight of His love. But learn to be at home in this darkness. Return to it as often as you can, letting your spirit cry out to Him whom you love" (chap. 3).

When we came to the monastery we answered yes to the question Benedict asks: are you truly seeking God? We answered yes but the search is still going on. It is still growing in our hearts. It develops into a "naked intent toward God in the depths of our being." This nakedness, this darkness, this absence, is really a fullness because we have found out who we are in the sight of God. Living under the Divine Gaze, we have come to ourselves,

---

49. St. John of the Cross, "The Spiritual Canticle, 1:12," *The Collected Works of St. John of the Cross*, trans. by Kieran Kavanaugh, OCD, and Otilio Rodriguez, OCD (Washington, DC: ICS Publications, 1973).

50. Ibid., I, 11.

51. Ibid., I, 12.

the true self. The inmost "I" is the perfect image of God. When this "I" awakens, we find within ourselves the Presence of him whose image we are.[52]

We will never truly know ourselves because where our "I" stops, God begins. This is a place of confusion and darkness for us now because it is too bright and our eyes are weak. But one day as we surrender ourselves to God in death, our eyes will be open to the deifying light and we will know as we are known.

Ordinary, Obscure, and Laborious Life

According to our Cistercian Constitutions, our life has been described as ordinary, obscure, and laborious (Constitution 3:5.) These are not good selling points. "Come join us in our ordinary and laborious life!" But when you get down to it, most people's lives are quite ordinary as well. If it were not so, there wouldn't be all those glamour magazines full of stories about the lives of the rich and the famous. In the doctor's office I sometimes pick up *People* magazine and glance at the articles about movie stars, rock musicians, and all the other glamorous people in the news these days. It amazes me to discover how much interest there is in stuff like this. Maybe the reason people buy these magazines is because their own lives are so ordinary, and they can live a more exciting life vicariously by keeping up with what the movie stars are doing.

But let's take a closer look at the description of our life. "Ordinary" means that we are able to occupy ourselves with things of the spirit, "laborious" prevents us from getting lazy, and "obscure" keeps us sharp and focused. We cannot settle down when something important in our life is obscure. We want to clarify it, get rid of the ambiguity and vagueness. If it is really important, we search for answers until we are satisfied. In other words, our ordinary, obscure, and laborious life keeps us searching.

---

52. Thomas Merton, *The Inner Experience: Notes on Contemplation* (New York: HarperSan Francisco, 2003), 15.

There are many things about life that are obscure—complicated systems and complex scientific phenomena we do not comprehend but can accept because we do not have to understand them to live with them. Almost everything that has to do with numbers, mathematics, chemistry, and for that matter science in general, is obscure to me. This does not matter because it is not essential that I understand it. If I had wanted to be a doctor, then it would have been a different story. But I have chosen a different direction for my life, as have all of us here at New Melleray. We have made the search for God primary in our lives. This is our passion, and for Cistercians it means choosing a way of life that is ordinary. In other words, there is not a lot of excitement here. Participating in the solemn blessing of our new icons at Vespers a few months ago was exciting, but it is not something that happens every week or every month or every year for that matter. I know many monks whose favorite days are the ferial days in Lent because they like the simple liturgy that focuses on the Gospel message of repentance. Our contemplative life cannot tolerate a lot of distractions. In fact, we have chosen to live in an enclosure—a cloistered life keeps out distractions. *Ora et labora*— prayer and work make up the rhythm of our days, and it is all very ordinary, all at the service of the inner life. Cassian says: "Those who are full jeer at the honeycomb." When our lives are filled with a lot of excitement we can easily forget about God. We lose our hunger and thirst for God. In his lengthy discourse on the prayer, "O God, come to my assistance, O Lord, make haste to help me," Cassian points out that the "poverty" of this phrase will keep us in close contact with God. In other words, we do not need a lot of diversity in our prayer. We do not need a lot of information in our reading. Instead, what may seem like a few poor words can form our hearts in the ways of prayer—"the poverty of the phrase." Such poverty keeps our minds sharp and hungry for more. It is a fasting of the mind, not the stomach.

When our life is ordinary it does not take much effort to find our way through the day. The monastic schedule carries us along. Also, on a more material level, our basic needs are provided for us. Our meals are prepared, our laundry washed, our income taken care of by the monastery, our medical bills paid—these are things most people spend many of their working hours providing for. Earning a living is a challenge. Our challenge lies elsewhere. Our struggle is to live the inner life of the spirit.

We know from history that many of the men who joined the original monastery at Citeaux were knights. Webb and Walker describe them like this: "From having been soldiers in the world, they dedicated themselves to spiritual warfare. . . . Being already formed in a noble military code . . . they had in effect only switched the battle into the level of 'psychomachia'—the fight for the soul. The enemy against whom they now had to take up arms was sensuality in her jeweled chariot, surrounded by her handmaids, frivolity, flirtation, carnal love and pleasure. . . . It was the Crusader against the Saracens fought on a higher plane of the individual's spiritual life. When it was done, the cleansed body and soul would become the holy of holies, a place where Solomon's Temple might be built anew and the Heavenly Jerusalem comes down and takes possession."[53]

St. Benedict uses a lot of military language in chapter 2, "On the Kinds of Monks." He talks about hand-to-hand combat, the battle line, the armor of obedience, taking up arms, doing battle with Christ. Thus even though our life is ordinary on one level, it is intense on the level of the spirit.

The obscurity of our life can be interpreted at different levels. On the one hand, our life is puzzling to many people who do not understand what it means to be a monk. We are often asked, "What is the purpose of your life?" No matter how carefully we try to answer that question, it is still hard for many people to comprehend. Why? Because the object of our life is obscure to us. Obscure means it is not readily understood. It is hidden, vague, and even dark. The dictionary says that in this context *dark* implies an imperfect or clouded revelation. God, the object

53. Webb and Walker, *Mirror of Charity* (London: Mowbray and Co., 1962), iv.

of our life, is obscure to us—hidden, not readily understood. I believe it was St. Hilary who said, "I have a firm grasp on something I do not understand." St. John of the Cross says faith is a night to our intellect. So yes, our life is obscure, hidden from others and even hidden from ourselves. It is difficult to live in an obscure place. Our intellects demand clarity. We cannot easily settle down or rest in obscurity, but such is the lot of all who live by faith and not by vision.

This is especially difficult for modern minds that have been formed by science. We are children of our culture and are accustomed to finding answers for every life situation. Our culture is good at this until it comes up against illness and death. Many people can live most of their lives in the obscurity of faith without realizing it. What shakes them out of their torpor is a life-threatening illness or the death of a loved one. Then they search for answers and find that what science and technology have to offer is of little help. It is only the certainty of faith that they are seeking, an answer that is more certain than science but more difficult to understand.

One of the temptations of monastic life is to settle for something less than God. It is to give up living in the cloud of unknowing. Our work can be a temptation in this regard, especially if it is rewarding and satisfying work. Our initial formation tries to teach us detachment in addition to responsible living with regard to work. I remember one postulant telling me he was leaving and going to look for a religious group where he could have more outdoor work. I have no doubt he felt a deep need for that, but it did not seem to be a good foundation on which to base his whole vocation.

It never works when we try to manipulate ourselves into certain jobs. It usually points to an escape from something essential in our lives as monks, a running from the ordinary, laborious, and obscure. The only way we can live in this manner is to keep ourselves centered in our search for God.

Enclosure as Formative Tool toward Wisdom

At the regional meeting held in Oka, Canada, in June of 2005, Dom Thomas Davis of New Clairvaux Abbey of Vina and Sr. Miriam Polard of Santa Rita presented a working paper about separation from the world. The paper was presented to the General Chapter in October of that year and contains much for us to learn or see anew.

At the heart of the paper was a summary of monastic enclosure that explained it not so much as a flight from the world but rather a flight into God. There is a different emphasis here. As Fr. Thomas has said, "We do not come to the monastery simply to be quiet in the most material sense, but through the ministry of that quiet, to enter into the redemptive depths of Christ's healing mission."[54]

Thus, enclosure is not merely a matter of observing separation from the world. Rather, it is fostered by the sense of *quies,* the stillness and silence in the heart. This *quies* is what is necessary for monastic prayer.

Now if we look at this as a backdrop for formation, we can make a similar statement. Enclosure is not an end in itself. It is at the service of the interior silence and stillness that leads us into interior prayer.

Formation is not a process we go through only during the first five or six years of our monastic life. True, it begins when we enter the monastery. But formation never ends because it has a multitude of goals. Initial formation is a movement from learning the external observances of monastic life to internalizing them as monastic values.

Perhaps I should have said there is a priority in our goals rather than a multitude of goals. One of the priorities in formation is to arrive at what is known as mystical wisdom. Although this sounds esoteric, it really is not. Anyone who has been in the monastery for some years has experienced it or at least longs for it.

---

54. *General Booklet for the General Chapter of 2005,* 32.

St. Bonaventure describes mystical wisdom as the suspension of the operation of our minds and the transformation of our affections. In other words, it is a surrender of our whole selves to God alone. St. Bonaventure says, "If you ask how such things can occur, seek the answer in God's grace, not in doctrine; in the longing of the will, not in the understanding; in the sighs of prayer, not in research; seek the bridegroom, not the teacher; God, and not man; darkness, not daylight; and look not to the light but rather the raging fire that carries the soul to God with intense fervor and glowing love."[55]

Our Constitutions say this a little more plainly: "Solitude, continual prayer, humble work, poverty, celibate chastity and obedience are not human skills and cannot be learned from human beings" (45:2). The first agent of formation in our Cistercian communities is the Holy Spirit. Next comes the community itself, and finally those who are directly involved in providing counsel and instruction, such as the abbot, the novice master, and teachers. Each has a role to play but everything is dependent on grace, not on the willpower of those involved.

What St. Bonaventure and our Constitutions are saying is that we have to place ourselves in the hands of God. Once we surrender ourselves, we find ourselves. We cannot do this on our own and no one else can teach us, because human skill is insufficient. When Bonaventure says the answer is in prayer, he is telling us we have to surrender our control, our will to have power over things.

The structure of our monastic day gives us many opportunities to make this surrender. If we give ourselves to the common life, for a while we are in darkness where someone else will lead us. Entering such a place is not easy to do. It takes a lot of trust. But if we fail to surrender we will never understand what Bonaventure is talking about. What is that goal that cannot be attained by doctrine, or understanding or research or daylight or even a teacher, but can be attained by prayer and darkness and

55. St. Bonaventure, taken from the Liturgy of the Hours, July 15.

desire and by going to the bridegroom rather than the teacher? I think the word "bridegroom" hints at the answer. "Bridegroom" speaks of a love relationship, and St. Bernard tells us that love is the only thing worthy of our human nature. We are made for love. Our Cistercian Fathers called the monastery a school of love. Our *Ratio* says of those in initial formation: "Through the discovery of the depths of God's mercy in their lives, they will learn to love."[56]

St. Bonaventure is talking about a stripping of our self. This is almost impossible unless we have experienced, at least a little bit, the new self, the true self, that is given to us. It is not attained by willpower. It is a gift that comes in prayer. It is the naked self standing before God with nothing to offer but our being, not our faculties or power but only our naked being, and having that being become one with God's being. "Thus each one lives in the other and is the other and both are one in the transformation of love," says St. John of the Cross.[57]

INTERIOR SILENCE AND FORMATION

Formation of the Heart

"May the spoken words of my mouth, the thoughts of my heart, win favor in your sight, O Lord" (Ps 18 [19]:15).

These words remind me of a statement St. Leo made when speaking of the Annunciation. He said words to this effect: "Mary conceived Jesus in her soul before she conceived him in her womb."

In both these texts, there is a visible and an invisible element. Mary conceiving Jesus in her soul is an invisible mystery while giving birth is visible. The thoughts of our hearts are invisible to others, but our spoken words are audible and can be comprehended by the senses.

56. *Ratio Institutionis*, no. 4.
57. St. John of the Cross, ibid., 12:6.

In formation we also have this visible and invisible duality. Formation, especially initial formation, is about learning how to behave like a monk. It is living the customs, the patterns, the schedule, the work, in a word, the culture of the monastery. It involves learning how we do things at New Melleray: how we live with each other, what we wear, what we eat, how we sing in choir, and all the daily routine at New Melleray. It does not take long to master these things. When we come to the intangibles, the spirit of New Melleray, it is a lot harder to figure out. Sometimes the only way to grasp the spirit of community is to visit another monastery. Oftentimes living so close to a thing makes it difficult to really see and fully appreciate it.

The novice master is supposed to discern if the newcomer is truly seeking God and is zealous for humility. This can sometimes be inferred from the novice's behavior. But it is harder to determine what is going on inside the novice. One cannot fully see the thoughts of his heart or the conception of the Word in his soul. These are invisible things. We could call this aspect of formation the "formation of the heart."

This phrase came up several times in the House Report at the 2005 General Chapter from Sujong, our monastery of Trappistine Sisters in Korea. The report states: "The annual retreat of 2004 was on 'Formation of the Heart.' This means Jesus' heart, that we should form our hearts to have the same emotion of Jesus." This reminds me of St. Paul's words: "Be of the same mind as Christ Jesus" (Phil 2:5).

Formation of the heart, or putting on the mind of Christ, is a lifelong process. Oftentimes the process is hidden from our own eyes. It reminds me of Bonaventure's words, "seek the darkness, not the daylight; seek the bridegroom, not the teacher."

Mary Magdalene and John the Baptist are two important figures in monastic spirituality. The significance of Mary lies in her ardent love, in her desire and seeking. The first reading for her feast day is taken from the Song of Songs. It is about the search, the longing, the desire for the bridegroom. There is a beautiful meditation on Mary sitting by the tomb on Easter Sunday, written by a thirteenth-century monk. It brings out the meaning of the formation of the heart. It begins: "Woman, why are you weeping? Who are you looking for? The one you seek is in your possession and you do not know it? It is within your inmost being and you look for it without? You stand outside, weeping at the tomb. Your heart is my tomb. And I am not dead there, but I take my rest in your heart. Your soul is my garden. You were right to suppose that I was the gardener. . . . I till and mind my paradise. Your tears, your love and your longing are all my work. In your inmost being you possess me, although you do not know it, and so you look for me without. Outwardly, therefore, I will appear to you, and so make you return to yourself that in your inmost being you may find the one whom you seek outside."[58] Hence, we may rightly say the formation of our hearts is a journey to return to ourselves.

The Eastern Fathers describe the deepest form of prayer as a descent into the heart. They speak of standing before God with the mind in the heart. This is not a descent from the mind, but a prayer of the mind in the heart. It is the reintegration of man's fallen nature, a restoration to original wholeness. It is an anticipation of heaven, and as such this prayer has an eschatological element to it.

The heart is the primary organ of our being. It is the very deepest and truest self, and the spiritual masters teach that it is not attained except through sacrifice and a dying to the false self. It is the absolute center, the innermost man. Here, at this point, we meet God. This is where the image comes face-to-face with the Archetype. Speaking of the heart, St. Macarius states, "God is there with the angels, light and life are there, the kingdom and the apostles, the heavenly cities and treasures of grace: all things are there."[59]

58. Andre Louf, *Teach Us to Pray* (Chicago: Franciscan Herald Press, 1974), 38–39.

59. Quoted in Kallistos Ware, *The Power of the Name* (Oxford: Fairacres Press, 1979), 17.

We can also express this by saying that our hearts are where Jesus is praying continuously to the Father. It is the true place of prayer within and never stops. Prayer of the heart is the living out of Paul's injunction to pray continuously. When the Orthodox monks speak of silence as the most important thing in prayer, they mean the silence that allows us to listen to the voice that is not our own and yet is our own. It is the voice of Jesus praying within us. The hesychist is the man of inner stillness, the one who transcends himself and enters into the mystery of prayer within his own heart.

Whether or not we experience this type of prayer is not that significant. What is important is that we believe in it. This is especially true at the liturgy. The Church teaches that the liturgy, the official prayer of the Church, is the prayer of Jesus to the Father. At the liturgy, the Eucharist, and the Divine Office, we participate in this prayer. Pope Pius XII taught this in his encyclical "Mediator Dei," and the teaching was repeated in the Constitution on the Liturgy of Vatican II: "Rightly then, the liturgy is considered as an exercise of the priestly office of Jesus Christ."[60]

When we pray the Divine Office, we are not doing so on our own. We are joining in the prayer of Jesus to the Father. It is the same prayer that is being offered in the hearts of all the baptized. When we participate in the Office it should not be with our distracted selves. We should each be in touch with our true self, our true heart and bring to the Office the prayer that is always going on within us. Essentially there is no difference between our private prayer and the public prayer of the liturgy. We pray with the same voice, the voice that is great within us.

Solitude of the Heart

The Gospel for Thursday of the Twenty-Fifth Week in Ordinary Time opens with the words: "Now it happened that Jesus was praying in solitude" (Luke 9:18). This notion of solitude is

---

60. *Constitution on the Sacred Liturgy*, no. 7.

echoed in the Decree of the Second Vatican Council on Religious Life, where we read, "Members of those communities which are totally dedicated to contemplation give themselves to God alone in solitude and silence" (*Perfectae Caritatis*, no. 7).

The model for this prayerful way of life is Jesus. It is Jesus praying on the mountaintop, Jesus spending nights in prayer, Jesus praying in the Garden of Gethsemane, and Jesus praying in solitude.

Solitude is an important element in our life. Distinguished from isolation, from reclusion and separation, solitude is defined as a situation in which a person is alone. In fact, some translations of Luke 9 read, "He was praying alone," instead of "in solitude." I like the word solitude better because it seems to have a deeper meaning than the word "alone."

To me, solitude brings a religious dimension into the picture. Jesus was praying in solitude. He was alone but that was secondary. That he was in solitude implies the outside world was shut out but the inner world was present. Imagine what Jesus' prayer in solitude was like. He was in deep communion with his Father. There is fullness in this solitude that promotes the fullness of communication. It is almost the opposite of being alone. We used to hear of the words, "Never less alone than when alone." It means that when we are alone we can give full attention to the spiritual presence, the presence of God. St. Benedict says we always live in *aspectu divinitatis*, in the sight of God.

The monastery is a rather complex mix of community life, togetherness, and solitude. There are all kinds of levels of communication taking place during the day in a monastery, from the frivolous to the most profound. There are also several degrees or levels of solitude. There is the solitude of being alone in your monastic cell. There is the solitude of moving about the monastery during the great silence, especially between Vigils and Mass. And there is the solitude of the heart that is always present. The heart that is given to God is reserved for God alone. It cannot be shared with another. Our vow of chastity is connected with this solitude of the heart. But in order for this to enhance rather than diminish our life, we have to keep reminding ourselves about the meaning of this solitude. It is for the sake of communication, for communion with God. It is based on Jesus praying in solitude. Jesus invites us into this prayer. In this way, even when we are praying together at the Office, our hearts are in solitude with God. This is one of the reasons we do not look around in choir. We try to give full attention to the prayer. After all, the Divine Office is the prayer of Jesus to the Father, and we are invited into that prayer. It is our mission in the Church to pray the prayer of Jesus for the salvation of the world. All have a role in the Mystical Body. The roles may differ, but it is all for the building up of the one Body of Christ.

St. Therese of the Child Jesus has a beautiful meditation on her struggle to find her role in the Church. She used St. Paul's analogy to the human body (1 Cor 12:12-26) and reasoned that every body needs a heart. Almost like a revelation, she saw her hidden life as the heart of the Church. It is the love that allows all other apostolates to function. Without love there would be no Mystical Body.

It might seem strange that Therese, a professed sister, would have to struggle with this question of her place in the Church. Did she not go through formation? Did she not know her Carmelite spirituality? She did, of course, but she did what all of us have to do: work out for ourselves how we understand our vocations and where they fit within the Mystical Body. Information and understanding are not the same thing. *Understanding* is closer to formation of the heart and no one, except the Holy Spirit, can do that for us.

Obedience "with a Good Soul"

In the early 1990s, one of our brothers, Br. Hilary Carney, died of a brain tumor. During his last weeks in the infirmary he would have night terrors, which is common to people suffering with that condition. He had a rather large picture of Christ the Lord of Divine Mercy on his bed stand. When terror would grip him, he would find peace by looking at this picture.

I think Br. Hilary was a monk who lived his vow of obedience in a way described by St. Benedict in the phrase *cum bono animo*. The Rule (RB 80) translates that phrase as "gladly," but I like the more literal translation: obedience should be given "with a good soul," or a good heart. In other words, with a good will. This can apply to our whole monastic life. Our Br. Hilary was a man who lived in the monastery with a good will. It is the only way to live. St. Benedict contrasts this with an obedience that is given grudgingly, by carrying out what is asked while silently grumbling about it. No one wants to live this way.

In the rite of solemn profession, we sing, "Receive me, Lord, according to your word, do not disappoint me in my hope." We all have expectations and hopes. Early on in the novitiate, we make a realistic appraisal of what we expect of the monastic life and what the community expects of us.

The monastic life is never exactly what one expects. There are many adjustments to be made in our thinking and living of the life. A good testing ground for one's ability to live the monastic life and be happy in it is found in chapter 5 of the Rule, "Obedience." In this chapter, St. Benedict presents a high ideal by depicting a monk whose vow to live a life of obedience is impelled by love. Benedict calls it "the narrow road that leads to life." Those who choose to follow it no longer live by their own judgment; rather they walk according to another's decisions and direction. This seems almost impossible to modern Americans. Our own judgments are sacred. No one tells us what to do! It is extremely difficult to give this up. In fact, we cannot do it on our own. We can only do it if it is our vocation, our calling from Christ to follow him in this way.

A monastic vocation is a gift, a gift of God to an individual and a gift to the Church. The gift is the grace to follow Christ, who said, "I have come not to do my own will but the will of him who sent me" (John 6:38). To give up our will to control everything, our will to power, has been described as the most difficult thing a modern man can do.

There is an ancient Chinese poem of only two stanzas that goes like this:

The birds have vanished into the sky
And now the last cloud draws away.
We sit together, the mountain and me
Until only the mountain remains.[61]

This is what happens to us in the monastic life. We disappear into Christ. His prayer becomes our prayer. His will becomes our will. His obedience, our obedience. His love of the Father possesses our love. We no longer live a separate existence. This is what we pray for at solemn profession. We ask three times not to be disappointed in our hope.

Patience Leads to Self-Transformation

During the Easter season, we celebrate the Resurrection of Jesus from the dead. But that is not all. We also celebrate his new state of being, the glorified body. In his glorified existence, Jesus reveals to us our own destiny. Not only do we believe in the resurrection from the dead but we also believe in sharing in the glorified body of Christ. We put on Christ, as St. Paul says. This means we become one with him in his new resurrected state, which is called his glorified body. We are clothed in his glory. Origen thus teaches that the goal of our transformation is the "spiritual body," the *soma psychikon*.

There is a lot of strong language used by the Fathers, especially the Desert Fathers about this self-transformation from the old self to the new self. One of the Fathers, Apollonius, says, "If I had not destroyed myself completely, I should not have been able to rebuild and shape myself again." Peter Brown, the famous historian of the early Middle Ages, says the motivation for sayings like this "was not hatred of the body but a profound desire to transform it into its original and blessed state."[62] It might be

61. Li Po, "The Birds Have Vanished," in *A Book of Luminous Things* by Czeslaw Milosz (New York: Harcourt, Brace, 1966), 277.

62. Quoted in Timothy Pettipiece, "The Desert as a Space of Transformation in Early Christian Spirituality," *Diakonia* 35, no. 2 (2002): 123.

more correct to say the state of the body after the Resurrection, not the blessed state before the fall.

Alexander Goylitsen says Cassian equates *apatheia* with purity of heart, the earthly goal of the monk. *Apatheia* is the stillness of our being at rest, the integration of our body, soul, and spirit energies. We know from experience how divided they can be and what turmoil our passions can cause us. Purity of heart comes from the purification of our life, the utter stillness that enables us to realize fully the implication of the Incarnation. We will attain this ultimately at the Resurrection.

The Desert Fathers have been called "semi-pelagians." In fact we were taught in the novitiate that Cassian is not a canonized saint in the Western Church because of this fear. I understand the word "semi-pelagians" to mean that there is a little too much emphasis on our own effort in the process of transformation. The Desert Fathers embarked on the way of *ascesis*—the way of ascetical practices—and because they appear to have put so much weight on them, we can get the impression that by practicing these disciplines we will become holy. We will attain *apatheia*. It is only the grace of Christ, however, that can attain these goals for us.

There was a time in our Trappist history when tremendous importance was attached to observances which were outlined in detail in a special book of regulations. Many of these observances came from La Trappe, others from Citeaux, and some go back to the Desert Fathers. A number of them came from the nineteenth-century French monasteries as well. But in recent years, our attitude toward these observances has changed dramatically. We could never be labeled semi-pelagians. We might come closer to a Lutheran understanding of faith alone. Good works are secondary. I say this to illustrate my point. I do think we are much more sacramental in our approach. The grace that comes through the sacraments is what sustains us. Our monastic practices are important but not absolutes. There is a balance between our sacramental life and our ascetical life.

One of our roles as monks is to keep the ascetical ideal alive by living it in the joy of the Resurrection, but the ideal changes as society changes. The third- and fourth-century monastic desert tradition was an adaptation to changing times. The Church that had been fiercely persecuted by the empire was gradually becoming the empire. As the age of the martyrs was coming to a close, the monks adopted a new and revolutionary approach to martyrdom, a kind of *martyrdom of the self* that would make a transformative union with Christ possible within the context of the contemporary historical situation.

This *martyrdom of the self* runs throughout the Rule of Benedict. Dying to self-will is taken as a primary value in the Rule, and the brief little sentence on patience is so important. St. Benedict says, "We shall through patience share in the sufferings of Christ that we may deserve also to share in his kingdom" (RB Prol. 50). He writes about the close connection between the passion of Christ, *passionibus Christi*, and our patient endurance, *per patientiam*. We participate in Christ's passion through our patience.

Here are the primary virtues in the Rule: humility, obedience, and patience. Patience is especially important in the cenobitic life where, as St. Benedict says, there is a great deal of variety in the personalities and characters of the men who are living closely together. In chapter 72, "The Good Zeal of Monks," he says we should "support the physical and moral defects of one another with the greatest patience." Patience is a martyrdom of the self. The Latin root *pati* means to "suffer." Patience is not just tolerance. Someone once said it is easy to be tolerant when you do not care.

Patience is a caring suffering, and we are all beginners when it comes to practicing it. Certain elements of our life together try our patience. It differs for each one of us. But there are things that drive us up the wall, things we would change if we could but we cannot. If you want a reality check, sit down and ask yourself, if you were abbot, what would you change? Come up with a list, and then follow through by planning how to implement your changes. You will at some point in your musings see how difficult or impossible it is to change or improve certain human situations. You just have to suffer them to be. It is through this suffering that we grow in likeness to Christ.

The problem is we can give up caring. It can be too exasperating. We can so easily say to ourselves, "Who cares! I do not care anymore. Let the community do what it wants. I have my own life to live." To care for the well-being of the community is to suffer. But if we do not, the community in the long run will become lifeless with no energy for caring for each other. Benedict gives us a beautiful ideal of community life. It is a life together focused entirely on God but at the same time caring for each other, serving each other as we would care and serve Christ himself.

Opportunities to Exercise Patience

Anything we do to foster unity in the community is a way of making present or actualizing the grace of the Eucharist. Anything we do to put to death sin and selfishness in our life is a way of sharing in Christ's sacrifice on the cross. In fact, we could say that any suffering we bear during the day is a way of sharing, or a way of making real, the sacrifice of Christ in our life.

Sharing in the sufferings of Christ is extremely important for us. Suffering is part of everyone's life—sometimes extreme, unwanted suffering, such as the death of a child, an announcement of terminal cancer, and all manner of unexpected turns of events that can catch us off guard.

As monks, we are called to guard our hearts, guard our thoughts, to shun forgetfulness. In this case, it could mean to be aware that painful events can come our way, and if they do they can be a way for us to share in the sufferings of Christ. By and through his cross, Jesus redeemed suffering. He makes it redemptive. Suffering can seem to be so impersonal, so random and happenstance. For us, it is eucharistic.

The phrase "Through patience we share in the sufferings of Christ" (RB Prol. 50) could be a whole way of life. It is difficult to think of a more important virtue for community life than patience.

I tried to come up with the many ways, or the many opportunities, we have to be patient. Remember, the Latin root of the word "patience" is *patio*—to suffer, to endure, to let it be. Each of you could come up with your own list, but here is mine:

1. We have to be patient when things are not going the way we think they should go. By this I mean work situations, liturgical situations, house discipline, the food we eat, the refectory book, the heat or lack of it in the house, the noise level, and a whole host of other things, great and small. Some of these can be pet peeves, some can be a matter of conscience. Several years ago a monk in another monastery announced he was no longer coming to the Office because the community was using a translation of the Psalms that had not been approved. For him, it was an issue of conscience. Most of our issues are not that extreme, but it happens occasionally that we are right, and we have legislation to back us up, and still nothing changes. The community might not be at the same place we are. All we can do is to be patient. Suffer it to be.

   Most often, it is the small things that get to us. When St. Benedict tells us to "support with greatest patience one another's weaknesses of body and behavior" (RB 72:5), he is giving us a lifelong struggle.

2. A second area calling for patience is with the abbot's ministry to the community or with what might be called his leadership style. I have often said that putting up with the foibles, failures, and defects of the superior is one of the big areas of asceticism for cenobites. When someone becomes abbot, his strengths and weaknesses become more apparent.

   It is the weaknesses that call us to patience. This applies to all areas of leadership, from the Abbot General's letters to the Acts of the General Chapter, to visitation or regional meetings. It is easy to criticize all these or dismiss them as irrelevant, but there is a word of truth coming to us here, even if it is just an occasion to practice patience.

3. Another big opportunity for practicing patience comes in the form of ourselves. If we experience no progress in our

spiritual life, we must be patient. We live in hope and in patience. We have to be patient with our failings—even in our sins.

Awareness of our failings and sins is one of the greatest graces we can receive. I mean this in the sense that it can lead to compunction, repentance, conversion, and compassion. Remember the Desert Father who carried a sack of sand in his arms? When asked why he did not sling it over his back for easier carrying, he replied that the heavy sack represented his sins. He always wanted to have those out front, so he could remember that he was a forgiven sinner. If he threw them over his back, he would forget about them and focus his attention away from himself and onto the failings of others.

Going deeper, we all struggle with the following sinful thoughts and actions: pride, greed, lust, gluttony, anger, envy, sloth, or *acedia*. Any one of these can put us under. We must be patient with our struggle. *Acedia* is especially difficult. It reveals itself in so many ways, such as boredom, lack of interest, wanderlust or restlessness, even joylessness. When we examine the seven capital sins, there is usually one or two that fit each of us in a special way. It is our struggle, and this is what calls for patience.

4. Finally, think of our vows. Think of how patience is interwoven with the practice of our vows, with obedience especially, as well as poverty, chastity, conversion, and stability. As we live out these vows each day, we have to be patient with ourselves and with the way others are living them in their daily lives.

We cannot live our lives out of a book. Instead, the book, be it the Bible, the Rule, or the Constitutions, shows us the way and gives us our ideals and values; but it is in the living of our ideals that the house is built. We can read the blueprints, but that is just the beginning. All of us are in the process of building our own houses. We are in the construction phase. We will not really see the beauty of the house until it is completed, until we hear the blessed words, "Come, you who are blessed by my Father. Inherit the kingdom prepared for you from the foundation of the world" (Matt 25:34).

OBSTACLES TO OVERCOME

Beware of "Acedia"

In the June 2004 issue of the *American Benedictine Review*, German scholar Christopher Joest wrote an interesting article on *acedia* and *apatheia*.[63] *Apatheia* is a state of interior peace. The battles are over, and one is calm within oneself. There is not a lot of interior noise or struggle. One is not a slave to his passions or compulsions or addictions. In one of his writings, Goylitsen calls it "purity of heart."

Joest treats *acedia*, which is one of the eight principal evil thoughts that plague the monk (the others are gluttony, lust, greed, sadness, anger, vainglory, and pride.) Not to be tormented by these thoughts and the vices to which they lead is to arrive at that state of inner freedom known as *apatheia*, or purity of heart.

Benedict does not mention *acedia* directly, but he does tell us to dash our evil thoughts against the rock that is Christ. In Institute 10, Cassian gives an extensive treatment of the eight principal thoughts and calls them the eight vices. These eventually became the seven capital sins.

There is a threefold division of these eight vices. The first three belong to the realm of the body; they are gluttony, lust, and greed. These attack the appetitive part of the soul. The middle three attack the emotion, or the irascible part of the soul. They

---

63. Christopher Joest, "Acedia and Apatheia," in *American Benedictine Review* (June 2004): 144.

are sadness, anger, and *acedia*. The last two are the most deadly because they belong to the realm of the spirit; these are vainglory and pride. Cassian says pride is like a prickly pear; no matter how you try to pick it up, you get stung. No matter how much we think we have succeeded in dealing with all the vices, we can always be stung with pride. At the root of all the vices is self-love; all the vices stem from this.

None of this is new to us. What might be new is the importance *acedia* plays in this scheme. It is very difficult to translate the Greek word *acedia*, which could mean grief, rage, resignation, boredom, weariness, despair, disgust, and self-pity.

You do not have to be in the monastery very long before you experience one of these realities. Depending on your temperament, *acedia* can affect you in a personal way. Boredom is my experience of it; others experience it differently. Joest says that it is a complex phenomenon that encompasses the other vices, especially sadness and anger: anger over what is there in the monastery, sadness over what is not there, what is missed.[64]

So when it relates to the monastic life in general, *acedia* is not just one temptation among many. It is quite simply *the* temptation of the monk, calling into question one's entire existence, the major identity crisis in which the foundations of everything are severely shaken.

Joest sees that this type of crisis is

> not just dealing with bad moods or psychic fluctuation or moral defects. It is a question of the resolve that arises in the wake of a decisive choice for which the monk risked his life and to which he must hold no matter what: to realize one's full potential in oneness with God. He has bet everything that he had and everything that he is on this.[65]

At solemn profession, we sing this phrase from Psalm118 three times: "Receive me, Lord, according to your word; do not disap-

---

64. Ibid., 145.
65. Ibid.

point me in my hope." Our hope is that we will truly be good monks and that the monastic life will bring us to our full potential as a human beings. In other words, we hope to be happy in the monastic life. I do not mean happy in a shallow sense but in a deep sense that, yes, this monastic path has blessed me with peace and contentment, and it fits me. No one can live the monastic life very long on willpower alone. There has to be a certain experience within the heart that indicates this is the right path.

Acedia is so dangerous because it makes us doubt our choice. It is a temptation to throw away everything and thus miss out on what matters most in the realization of our full potential of union with God. It worms its way into the inner chamber of our hearts and casts doubts about the genuineness of our vocations. It slowly creeps in, and with the passing of time, erodes our interior certainty.[66]

Evagrius, who was the first to outline the eight evil thoughts, traces all kinds of problems in the monastic life to their roots in *acedia*. These include fear of sickness, anxiety over old age, memories of our former way of life, the observances of the brothers, arrogance in dealing with the brothers, and others we might not readily recognize as being connected to *acedia*. Evagrius says these thoughts are like demons that wage war on certain parts of the soul, but the demon of *acedia* tries to suffocate the whole soul. It is a temptation to give up the struggle. When that happens we can do one of two things: either give up our vocation entirely or make a little niche for ourselves where we try to survive with as much comfort as possible. In either case, we give up the struggle.

In his treatise on the eight principal vices, Evagrius gives fifty to sixty thoughts that characterize this particular demon. In each case, he cites a passage from the Sacred Scriptures to use in fighting the evil thoughts. Joest comes up with five summary points of Evagrius' thoughts:

---

66. Ibid., 144, footnote nos. 100 and 101.

1. *Pointlessness*: a hatred for work and a sense that the monastic life is pointless, a feeling that there must be something easier and that suffering and *ascesis* itself are meaningless.

2. *Discouragement*: a feeling of helplessness and grief, a sense of desolation and misery because of sickness or hardship, a temptation to give in to grumbling and dissatisfaction.

3. *Hatred of the brothers*: this can be directed at the superior as well as the other monks and sometimes surfaces in the form of an attempt to find false consolation among others in the community.

4. *Thoughts of flight*: this manifests itself in the desire to leave the cell and the monastery in order to return to the world and to one's relatives.

5. *Miscellaneous*: a fading of the inner light and an attempt to put one's confidence in one's own power instead of God. There are no tears of repentance.

In other words, *acedia* can be summarized as the temptation to give up! *Acedia* can affect young monks as well as older ones. There are days when we are tempted to give up the struggle and take another path, either outside or inside the monastery.

The remedy for *acedia* is patience, and it plays a huge role in our monastic life. By it, says St. Benedict, we share in the suffering of Christ. We suffer things to be as they are; and yet terrible as that might be, we do not let it divert us from our goal of perseverance. "Persevering" literally means "remaining under." We remain under our vows, we suffer them, we submit to the demands made on us by our monastic vows. Evagrius says, "What heals *acedia* is staunch persistence and doing everything with much attentiveness and fear of God."

The monk, then, should continue to work at a task and not allow himself to be taken away from it by the variety of distractions that crop up. If we guard our thoughts by being attentive to God, the evil thoughts which lead to evil actions will not find a home in us.

Fighting the Evil in Our Thoughts

There was a large turnout for Fr. John Michet's talk on demonology and exorcism when he visited New Melleray in 2004. He is the official exorcist for the Archdiocese of Chicago. I was curious why so many had come, and several possible explanations came to mind. First of all, demonology played an important role in the New Testament; Jesus often drove out demons. This awareness of the presence of evil is carried over into the early monastic life. The Desert Fathers had a vivid and daily experience of the demons. Talk of the devil and demons brings us back to one of the sources of our spirituality.

A second point is that we have all but forgotten this source. When someone comes and reminds us, we are very interested in hearing more about the topic. Fr. Michet represents a very modern approach to demonology; to hear what he had to say about the devil touched a nerve with us. We just do not talk that way, but hearing Fr. Michet made us think about our own approach to the devil. He pointed out that it can be difficult to discern cases of demonic possession, whether it is the devil or our own weak self that is involved. When it comes to exorcism, discernment is essential; it is at the very heart of the matter. What is really going on here? Fr. Michet said that out of a hundred possible cases, only four would most likely be true cases of possession.

The office of exorcist is an official one in the Church. It used to be one of the minor orders along with lector and door keeper. It has been lost in our modern Church, where it seems the dark side of life, including sin, guilt, the devil, and evil, has been demythologized out of existence. It reminds me of a statement Archbishop James Byrne made about a book entitled *Whatever Became of Sin?* written by the psychologist Karl Menninger. The archbishop felt it should have been written by a theologian rather than a psychologist. The common practice of the Church today is not to put too much emphasis on guilt and sin. Maybe there was an overemphasis before, but to deemphasize does not mean to ignore.

Be that as it may, we in the monastery cannot cast a condemning eye on the practices of the modern Church. We have our own spirituality to care for, and this brings us back to the question of how we understand the place of the devil in our modern monastic life. I cannot possibly answer that question entirely, but I can offer some of my own observations.

We begin with some illustrations from the life of St. Benedict. I remember two instances reported by St. Gregory that reveal St. Benedict's wise discernment and his ability to see what others could not about why people behaved the way they did.

There is a story about a monk who used to wander off from the community at the time of silent prayer. They must have had common meditation in Benedict's day, just as we used to have after Vigils and Vespers, and this particular monk had a habit of leaving the common prayer and wandering off. As Gregory says, "He passed the time aimlessly at whatever happened to interest him." This is not such a farfetched story. I have seen monks like this, and I can easily see myself doing the same thing now and then. But to get back to the story, the abbot used to correct the wayward monk, and he would reform for a while, but then fall back to his old ways. Again, this is not so hard to imagine. Finally, his abbot asked Benedict for some advice, and so Benedict visited the monastery. Sure enough, after the Psalmody and just as the silent prayer began, off went the monk. To make a long story short, Benedict was the only one who could see what was really happening. He saw a little demon pulling at the edge of the monk's habit, leading him out of church. Benedict followed the monk out, found him loitering about and hit him with his crosier! Bingo, just like that the monk straightened up! Gregory ends the story with the words, "It was as if that ancient enemy had been struck by the blow himself and was afraid to domineer over the monk's thoughts any longer."

Did Benedict really see a demon pulling on the monk's habit? I do not know. Does Fr. Michet really see all the things he reported? I do not know, but the essence of the story is in the last sentence: "The demon was afraid to domineer over the monk's thoughts anymore." This is what Benedict really saw; he discerned the real situation. The monk was not acting totally on his own. His thoughts and his actions were being influenced by the evil one.

Here is an entry way for us to better understand the role of evil in our life, especially in our thinking. We have to exorcise our thoughts many times during the course of a day. This is a basic practice of monastic life. Evagrius, the first to delineate the seven major thoughts that assail monks, also offered an antidote for each of them. Fasting, for example, became a way to deal with gluttony. The monastic life, like a hospital, was a place to be restored to health by being given a practice to heal the soul and help the monk reach inner peace and tranquility of heart. I like the way the book of Proverbs says the words of Scripture are "health for our being" (Prov 4:22). We all know what physical and psychological health is, but many people neglect spiritual health, health for their being. We have all struggled with evil thoughts. We have all at one time or another given into them. Where sin is involved, we have to believe the devil is involved as well.

We have been redeemed by Christ and washed clean in his blood, but we are still *in via*; that is, we have not yet fully attained our salvation. It is ours if we choose it, but there is still within us a propensity, a pull, or concupiscence toward sin. The ancient monks were very much aware of this tension. They realized that our life is a battleground, or a place of struggle. Benedict outlines this in Chapter 1 of his Rule, where he describes the various kinds of monks. The hermits and the cenobites are engaged in a struggle, and Benedict refers to it as a battle line, a hand-to-hand combat. The gyrovagues and the sarabaites are not. They might seem healthy and happy, but they have given up and are seeking a life of pleasure by doing their own will and not living under the direction of another, as Benedict says the cenobites do.

During the day, we make many choices in the secret of our hearts to do good and avoid evil. Choices like this begin in our thoughts; no one but God sees these choices that originate in our minds. No one but God sees how much we might entertain evil thoughts.

Year after year, if we choose to do good and avoid evil, Christ is being formed in us. Our lives take on the character of an icon bearing the features of Christ through us. We are painting the icon by the choices we make. Our lives are a creative labor; we have chosen to be monks, to make this our life's creative work. By taking the monastic habit, we embrace the whole long tradition of monastic living. We do not need to read everything written about monastic life. Everything written, every word expressing our tradition will be played out in us by practicing the life. One of the major practices will be our struggle with the evil one as he tempts us with our own thoughts. Jesus went out into the desert, the habitat of demons, to subdue them; we follow in his footsteps. I like what Fr. Michet had to say about this: "Have no fear." We have the most powerful weapon, the power of the name of Jesus. The repetition of the name of Jesus wards off all evil. It brings peace to the soul. It is, as Bernard says, oil poured out, a balm sweeter to the tongue than honey from the comb.

HUMILITY AND EXALTATION IN CHRIST

Compunction and Compassion

As we progress in the monastic life, we move from complexity to simplicity in the way we live our lives. By this, I do not necessarily mean external simplicity, although ideally, internal and external simplicity should be intimately related.

I am speaking more of inner simplicity as related to our prayer lives and our understanding of our monastic spirituality. Most of us have been here long enough to know what works for us and what does not. It might be ideal to spend an hour a day in *lectio divina*, but this is not always possible. Some might prefer the rosary or the Stations of the Cross to a more traditional practice. I suppose the criterion is what works for us, what resonates with who we are.

We have a lot of freedom in choosing what to read or how to pray. As we mature, we become more certain the Holy Spirit has spoken to us and guided us to where we are and the choices of practices that appeal to us. Each individual may be drawn to a different practice, which may be studying and teaching theology, praying the rosary, pure *lectio divina*, silent meditation, the Mass and the Office, or even work as a form of prayer. When we are new in the monastic life, we try on different clothes to see what fits us. It takes years to find the right fit. The strange thing is that what we settle into might not be what the book says it should be. What works for each of us within the parameters of monastic life is what the Holy Spirit has directed us to embrace.

Within this freedom, however, there are certain fundamental principles of the monastic life that have to be present if one claims to be a monk. It would be interesting to draw up a list of fundamentals. Charity is certainly one principle, service to the community is another.

There is one fundamental of our life that is not so easy to remember, much less to practice. It is compunction, repentance, sorrow for sin, or awareness of unworthiness. This basic principle is expressed in a saying of the Desert Fathers: "It is better to convert our own souls than to convert a multitude of heathens." There is another saying: "The less a monk thinks about converting the world and the more he thinks about converting his own soul, the more likely the world will in fact be converted."[67]

There are several reasons for the importance of this way of thinking. Probably most importantly, it keeps us from judging our brothers. St. Augustine says, "Men are strange creatures, the less they focus on their own sins, the more they focus on the sins of others." Not to judge others is a primary rule of the cenobium. After all, we live like a family here. Everyone sees what everyone else is doing. There are very few secrets among us.

When we see something that we think is not right, we are quick to judge the individual involved. You might say this is the way of the world that we bring into the monastery when we

67. Bishop Kallistos Ware, "Seek First the Kingdom," *Theology Today* (April 2004): 24.

enter. To withhold judgment is very difficult. The trouble is we see only the appearances. God sees the heart. We do not know the struggles that are going on in the hearts of our brothers.

There must be hundreds of Desert Fathers' sayings that forbid us to judge our brother. The best way to do this is not by making a firm resolution not to so act, as if willpower alone could achieve this. The best way to keep from this vice of judging others harshly is to be acutely aware of our own failings and sins. Hold them like a sack in front of our face, not like a sack slung against our back. On our back, we might forget they are there. In front of our eyes, we cannot forget them.

This leads to another reason for the importance of compunction. It keeps us from forgetting who we are. We can easily wander into the level of forgetfulness by setting aside the darker side of our life. We are told to shun forgetfulness and live in the presence of God with our whole self, not just the part of our self that we like and want to show to people. But if we can have our whole self in our hands and accept who we are, we will then of necessity be men of humility. The ancients used to love to string the virtues together and show how they are related. Compunction and humility are the bedrock of cenobitic monastic life.

Yet there is another dimension to this. It is our relationship with ourselves. Guilt is part of our nature. We have to deal with it. It is not an easy balance to achieve. Either we have too much guilt and become discouraged or angry about it, or we feel no guilt at all and become coarse of heart or hardhearted. We hope to carry the verse of this psalm in our hearts, not as a discouragement but as a revealed truth: "In guilt I was born, a sinner was I conceived. You love truth in our heart; in my inmost heart teach me wisdom" (Ps 50:7-8).

The truth in our heart is that we are guilty of sin. From that truth comes wisdom by way of forgiveness. We cry out for forgiveness, not just for ourselves but for all people. The chain of virtue grows. Compunction leads to humility, humility to mercy, mercy to forgiveness. This is the wisdom we are taught not from books but from experience, from life, from a true evaluation of who we are before God.

This type of wisdom comes with age. I remember a talk given at the General Chapter by the senior abbot, Amandus of Tegelen. He was about eighty at the time and had been an abbot for over thirty-five years. The whole talk was on mercy. It was not the topic he was assigned, but it is what he spoke about, namely, the need for mercy and forgiveness in our dealings with each other and with ourselves. This is not much different from St. Bernard's teaching about self-knowledge. That is the first thing we learn about ourselves when we come to the monastery: self-awareness of who we are before God. This gives birth to compunction of soul and leads to compassion, which results in our desire to treat our brothers with mercy. Our self-awareness teaches us that we are all in the same position before God. We are all weak, but we have all been forgiven.

Compunction is the foundation for the ladder of humility. St. Benedict tells us the beginning of humility is fear of the Lord. This is the salutary fear or awe as the goodness of God penetrates into the guilt of our heart, and we still live. We are not destroyed by the goodness but washed clean and embraced by it. What we deserve and what we receive are so different. As high as the sky is above the earth, so far does he remove our sins.

We are washed and made clean and we should never forget that this comes only from the mercy of God, not from our own merits. If we always remember this, we will know that we cannot condemn our brother. We must forgive as we have been forgiven.

Striving for the Selfless Love

The House Reports for the 1996 General Chapter focused on the theme of "The Community, School of Charity." Prior to this chapter, Abbot General Dom Bernardo issued a circular letter which focuses on chapter 72 of the Rule of St. Benedict, especially on the phrase in verse 7: "No one is to seek what is useful for himself, but rather what is useful for the other" (RB 72:7).

At the conclusion of his letter we read: "Unfortunately, our hearts are never free of mercenaries who traffic selfishly with God and neighbor, nor are there any lack of bachelors and old maids who have made themselves the center of their universe, displacing God and neighbor."

The word "bachelor" caught my attention. The Abbot General uses it in a derogatory sense, but the word itself is neutral. The Abbot General weighs it down with a lot of negativity. He uses it to describe a monk who is just an unmarried man caring for no one but himself. Unfortunately, this is a reality in our life. There is a real temptation to become bachelors who happen to live together. The Abbot General's antidote to this poison is to seek to do what is good for others rather than for ourselves. This may, of course, be correct, but it is easier said than done. I think it is more complex than that.

I have been reading an article in *Theological Studies* called "The Broken Wings of Eros: Christian Ethics and the Denial of Desire."[68] The author, Peter Black, establishes the importance of eros in our lives. He goes so far as to say, "A life solely of selfless, self-forgetting, self-sacrificial agape would be deficient." This kind of thinking takes you aback, because this type of agape/love is what Benedict is advocating when he says to put other interests before our own. He is, of course, quoting St. Paul.

The Abbot General has reminded us that we must accept this as a whole program of life. I agree, and I also feel there is a whole lot of integration that has to happen before we arrive at this type of total self-giving love, this agape, the disinterested love.

Forgetting this integration or ignoring the steps leading to selfless love is one of the reasons there can be bachelors instead of monks living in the monastery. We cannot begin our journey to God by assuming we have already arrived at its destination. There are stages of growth that must be taken into consideration. We cannot cut off part of our life and expect to be whole persons. It is the old dilemma of how can you give yourself totally to the monastic way of life if you do not have a self to give.

---

68. Peter Black, "The Broken Wings of Eros: Christian Ethics and the Denial of Desire," *Theological Studies* 64, no. 1 (March 2003): 106–26.

Eros and agape are two forms of love and both are needed. We tend to reduce eros to sensual love, but it is much more than that. It is, among other things, the driving force behind "falling in love," and this can be a wonderful experience. It usually does not last a lifetime, but it is important in establishing a permanent relationship. The sexual element is only part of the picture. There is also delight in simply being with the other person, a sort of preoccupation with the other. There is true self-forgetting and generosity involved. Usually this is not a permanent state, because in the beginning the two people involved tend to idolize each other. They idolize this form of love. They can be in love with love because of the good feeling it brings. They often love the other person because of what they themselves are receiving from him or her. Trying to find completion in the other never lasts long. It can be a messy business, but it can also be a necessary element in psychological development.

Self-love is an ambiguous term. We are told that it is selfish, but then we are also told to love our neighbors as ourselves. I suppose you could say there is a healthy self-love and an unhealthy self-love.

Healthy self-love is described as

> a self-love that overcomes self-hate or loathing and can integrate our good tendencies into a positive direction for our lives. It affirms dynamisms in ourselves that foster our identity and help us reject those dynamisms that lead to disintegration. (This would be things like obsession, compulsion or addiction.) We have a duty in fact of self-love because what is at stake is our positive self-identity. A consequence of such a healthy self-love is that you do not have to denigrate, use or parasitically identify with the goodness of others as ways of bolstering a sense of your own self-worth.[69]

Self-love lies behind our concern for our own personal integrity and identity.

69. Ibid., 116.

A healthy sense of self, a strong sense of who we are, and a strong ego are a good foundation for monastic life. The common life can bring out the best and the worst in us.

Traditionally, we are taught to move out of eros toward agape. Eros is the love we have for someone or something because of what they do for us. Agape is love of another just for their sake alone, not because of some benefit we receive in return. This is really not the case however. Eros is a real form of love. We can try to go beyond it, but we can harm ourselves by trying to live without it. Without it, our life would have no passion, no enthusiasm, no energy, and even no creativity. It is the source of desire. The article "Broken Wings of Eros" refers to a type of spirituality that cuts off eros, that tries to bypass it. This is a dangerous approach. It produces self-centered bachelors and old maids.

We are speaking of two approaches to monastic spirituality. One is suspicious of eros, while the other seems to embrace it. One stresses detachment or denial of desire and the power of the intellect. The other emphasizes attachment, the release of desire, feeling, and the body.

The article quotes Joan Timmerman as saying,

> It is not the renunciatory lifestyle that produces grace, but the response to grace that takes forms sometimes of detachment and sometimes of attachment. In the history of spirituality, detachment has been interpreted as having greater intrinsic value, but the movement of the Spirit toward embodiment, engagement, and of taking hold are fruits equally of grace. . . . Certain approaches to spirituality, those stressing detachment, control, the rational, and suspicion of the body and emotions have also helped to clip the wings of Eros. Contrasting French and German spirituality, Emmanuel Levinas suggests that German spirituality draws on Eros while French spirituality does not. To the contrary, a German, with his sensitivity, is interested in this inner drama, this blind-to-reason, unyielding restlessness. Germans see in it the richness and the depth of the human spirit. Understanding the spirit of man does not mean knowing

the soul of man by reason, but rather living without trying to escape from life. Does a spirituality that escapes from the arrow of Eros also aim to escape life?[70]

Living without trying to escape from life is what Jesus did in the desert. This is also what Lent is all about.

The Abbot General's remarks about our monasteries having enough bachelors, old maids, and sarabites (people who do their own thing) comes true when we try to reach full unselfish love without going through some of the necessary stages of growth. It is similar to Erikson's stages of growth where the final stage is generativity. You do not arrive at this when you are twenty years old. It comes at a later stage. We cannot begin with disinterested love. Our first years in the monastery are similar to a couple falling in love and then after some years, dealing with the realities of their relationship. I remember having many of the symptoms of being in love as a postulant and novice, only the object of my love was the monastic way of life, the externals of it. I think it is a necessary stage, a passion for the life.

We cannot live very long as neophytes, but on the other hand, we do not want to lose our passion for the monastic way of living. Each one of us has to find a particular element in our life that becomes our main story, be it *lectio*, the Office, meditation, the Jesus Prayer, service to the community, or something else we have passion about.

There is another thing that is most helpful and that is our personal devotion to the Lord Jesus. This can be a very important devotion that keeps us human, that embraces our affective life.

Holding up the Ideal before You

A mature monk has found a way to internalize certain aspects of the life that nourish him and support him in his journey. Most of us have found one or two things that form the basic

70. Ibid., 121.

structure of our life, like the Liturgy of the Hours, *lectio*, the rosary, or work. Some find one practice more spiritually nourishing than the other. If, for example, you prefer to say the rosary rather than *lectio divina*, then that is it. There is no use trying to fit yourself into a slot that does not work for you.

We all use this private approach in one way or another, but one of the dangers with it is that we can deceive ourselves. For instance, we might say that the liturgy is where we are truly able to be ourselves, where we feel we are being nourished, and yet our actions may reveal another message. I remember years ago hearing one monk complain that we were not doing anything together anymore, yet he was always absent whenever we did! So who we are and who we think we are can be two different things.

This is why it is important to have the ideals of monastic life presented to us frequently. It gives us an opportunity to take a look at where we are in order to measure ourselves against the ideal. We might not match up, but it is important that we take the ideal seriously enough to dialogue with it and work out an acceptable way to live it. We read a passage of the Rule every day in the refectory. It is a reminder, a call to reflect. It is the same with the readings we hear each day at the Divine Office and the Eucharist. They form us, and they also challenge us. We have to have some sort of answer to the question of how the way we live corresponds to the teachings of Jesus and the teachings and tradition of our Benedictine and Cistercian life.

I believe one of my ministries as abbot is to hold up before you the ideal, even if it simply means repeating passages from the Rule or the Constitutions. These are documents that articulate our monastic ideal, our vision of life.

Monastic life is nothing if it is not practical. We do not speculate about the monastic life; we practice it. This does not mean we live it unreflectively. We should reflect on our practice and dig into it in order to gain better understanding and deeper insight. Action and reflection have to go together. We cannot be like the monk who could not come to the liturgy because he was writing a paper on the liturgy. Whatever we write or speak should be an articulation of our experience, our practice, and our observance, not just a serving up of something we read in a book.

We as individuals and communities live in the context of our Cistercian patrimony. Our Cistercian Fathers are speaking about our experiences though we are separated by almost a thousand years. They are channels of grace for us because they have the gift of teaching and writing about our life. They can express things that we may intuit only dimly or vaguely. Once we read a sentence, it can open up a new place in our life, or at least shine a light on something we knew but needed to hear in a new way.

This happened to me when I was searching for something to read at Lauds for the feast of Blessed Guerric. Two sentences from his homily on the Resurrection caught my attention. He says, "It is much more important to receive Jesus in our hearts than to see Him with our eyes or hear Him with our ears. The Spirit makes a much deeper impression on the interior man than material things make on the exterior senses" (Sermons 33.4). I think that it is a valid form of *lectio* just to take a passage like that and stay with it for a while, even if you put the book away and never return to it again.

This passage can help us understand one of our ideals. I refer to the constellation of practices centered on simplicity, renunciation, withdrawal, guarding our thoughts, enclosure, liturgy, and even the use of the media. Take liturgy, for example; Cistercian liturgy is not parish liturgy. Ours is more austere, simple, and repetitious. The reason for this is contained in the words of Blessed Guerric: "The Spirit makes a deeper impression on the interior man than material things on the exterior senses." Our liturgy is interspersed with periods of silence. We do not have a lot of new music. Our Divine Office in fact is very repetitious. We have the same psalms and the same antiphons over and over. The focus is on God, not us, but insofar as we are engaged, it is on the level of the Spirit. We do not try to stimulate or, should I say, overstimulate our senses.

The principle enunciated by Guerric can be applied to many elements of our life. Cassian says, "Those who are full jeer at the honeycomb." In other words, we have to keep our life somewhat empty in order to appreciate the sweetness of the Scriptures. Maybe this is why St. Benedict comes down so hard on overindulgence, or as one translation has it, surfeiting. Overindulgence dulls our spiritual appetite. For this reason, the whole life of a monk should have a Lenten quality about it. This principle applies so much to the use of the media. We have restrictions on the use of TV, videos, and the internet, not because these things are evil but because they appeal so powerfully to our senses. They occupy us at a level that is overdone (overindulgence again) and they destroy the emptiness needed to enter our interior world.

So many of our ascetical practices can seem negative if we miss the meaning of why we practice them. It is as if we were experiencing only the negative half of the equation, and no one can live a fruitful life merely from a negative perspective. Guerric is showing us the positive side of the equation: "It is more important to receive Jesus in our hearts than to see him with our eyes." Our senses can get in the way in fact.

To receive Jesus in our hearts, we have to put our senses to sleep as it were, or at least restrict their normal intake. But we cannot do this with willpower alone. In order to be fully developed human beings, we need to experience the positive side of our ascetical practices. We have to receive Jesus in our hearts. To read about him in the Gospels, to study him in theology is not enough. We wish to receive him in our hearts. If this happens, then to see him with our eyes or hear him with our ears can be a distraction. After all, the apostles saw him and heard him but did not truly receive him in their hearts until Pentecost. Then they were set on fire for love of him.

Depriving our senses, then, through fasting, vigils, restricting the use of the media, simplicity of life, and poverty at all levels is at the service of receiving Jesus in our hearts. This one phrase from Blessed Guerric is the context of a whole way of life. Without this experience, we will grow weary of asceticism and make many compromises. With the experience, everything will flow naturally, our hearts will expand, and we will run in the way of salvation.

Call to Perfection

The conversion story of St. Francis reminds me of the conversion story of St. Anthony, the Father of Monks. Both men were moved by the same passage of Scripture: the story of the rich young man as recounted in Matthew 19:16-22.

These conversion stories were not stories of moving from no faith to faith; both Francis and Anthony were baptized Christian Catholics. Their conversion was from the state of being a Christian to another more intense form of belief. Both were moved by Jesus' words, "if you will be perfect." The word "perfect" in Greek (*telaios*) means "mature or complete" in one's discipleship. Jesus tells the rich young man, "You have been doing well in following the law, but if you want to be complete, sell what you have and come, follow me." He is telling him, "Dispossess yourself and follow my path."

The rich young man could not make such a sacrifice because even though he followed the law, he was still very much attached to his possessions. Anthony and Francis did make the sacrifice. They took the Lord at his word. They literally gave up whatever they owned and followed the Lord as they understood his call.

This passage from Matthew (Matt 19:21) is one of the foundations of religious life in the Church. The dispossession is entailed in the vows of poverty, chastity, and obedience. St. Ambrose (335–397) was the first one to explain this text by distinguishing between precepts and counsels. He said that there are two ways of commanding things; the first is by precepts, and the second is by way of counsels. The fact is that Jesus gave the rich young man a counsel, not a command. The precepts in the story are the command to love God and love your neighbor. All Christians have to do this. The counsel was to sell everything and follow Jesus. This applies to all who live the life of the evangelical counsels.

The Decree on the Appropriate Renewal of the Religious Life of the Second Vatican Council is known as *Perfectae Caritate*. These Latin words are based on Matthew 19. Perfect charity or perfect love is shown by leaving all to follow Christ. That is what we do by entering religious life and professing the vows. It is meant to be a total self-giving, a dispossession, selling all, and following Christ. It is our response to Jesus' request as told in Matthew 19. The Gospel passage is relived every time someone professes vows. Others may live out the precepts and counsels in another way, but the traditional teaching of the Church is that the religious profess to follow Christ by giving up the radical right to own anything.

It seems to me that there are two parts to Jesus' request. There is the initial desire to follow Christ—the interior prompting, the initial impulse. Then there is the actual putting into practice the counsel to sell all.

Let us look for a moment at each of these. After hearing the young man explain himself, Jesus invited him to go a step further, and make a greater sacrifice. He was indeed living a good life; he could have stayed where he was. In fact, he was the one making the inquiry of Jesus. He started the conversation. Jesus outlined a good life for him, and the young man said, "I am doing all that. What do I still lack?"

This conversation, this short dialogue, took place during Jesus' life on earth but it is still going on today. We are in this conversation with Jesus; it is really a call to conversion. The rich young man asked Jesus, "What am I still lacking?" It is a question we should always ask, as St. Bernard frequently asked himself, "Bernard, why did you come here?" Questions like this keep us focused.

Baldwin of Canterbury has beautiful insights about the power of the word of God:

> When this word is preached, in the very act of preaching, it gives to its own voice which is heard outwardly a certain power which is perceived inwardly. . . . The Word then is alive in the heart of the Father, on the lips of the preacher, and in the hearts of those who believe and love Him.[71]

71. Baldwin of Canterbury, taken from the Liturgy of the Hours, Friday of the Thirtieth Week in Ordinary Time.

When we hear the Word proclaimed both in the readings and in preaching, through them we enter into a life-giving conversation with the Risen Lord. The Word is meant to penetrate to the deepest recesses of our being. Baldwin says,

> When this word is spoken, its message pierces the heart like a sharp arrow . . . like nails driven deep; it enters so deeply that it penetrates to the innermost recess. This word is as such more piercing than any two-edged sword, inasmuch as it is stronger than any courage or power, sharper than any shrewdness of human ingenuity, keener than all human wisdom, or the subtlety of learned arguments.[72]

It is this living Word that inspires men and women to make vows of poverty, chastity, and obedience, to leave all and follow Christ.

After the desire comes the practice. St. Francis mentions the teaching and footprints of the Lord. The footprints are the practices, walking the same path as Jesus. It is important in our doing of the Word, or in our living out the vows, to stay close to the initial experience of the call, the initial experience of the Word piercing and penetrating our hearts. If we leave this behind, our practice will grow lukewarm, even cold. We will be going through the motions but without heart, without soul.

The way we stay close to the original fire is by *lectio divina*, by meditating and contemplating the Word spoken to us in the liturgy and in our private prayer. We cannot sustain one without the other. If we are not doing *lectio*, the center of our life collapses, and we lose the heart of our life. If we are doing *lectio* but not putting it into practice, it is just an intellectual exercise, a curiosity rather than a piercing of our hearts.

The decree *Perfectae Caritate* tells us that "the more ardently they [the religious] unite themselves to Christ through self-surrender involving their entire lives, the more vigorous becomes the life of the Church and the more abundant her apostolate bears fruit" (PC, par.1).

72. Ibid.

Dispossession Is to Live by the Lord's Strength

In the concluding prayer at None on the Saturday before the First Sunday of Advent, the hebdomadary prays that "we may live by your strength, O Lord." That we may live by your strength—this implies we are not living by our own strength.

Our document on formation called *Ratio* states: "The monasticate continues and complements the work of the novitiate in a way that is less structured and which is spread over a longer period. During it the juniors will progressively learn to act more from inner principles and more towards a fuller participation in the activities and responsibilities of the community" (no. 39). What stands out for me is the following passage: "Learn to act more from inner principles." There is a type of progression here; when we first come to the monastery, during those first months and even years, we learn the external patterns of the monastic life. We learn the horarium, the various work assignments, the layout of the buildings, the farm, and the surrounding fields and forest. A retreat master emphasized once that as a lover of the place, a monk should know every square inch of the monastery property and buildings. This takes time, just as it takes time to learn all the behaviors and practices of monks. But gradually, toward the end of the novitiate and into the juniorate, one is expected to internalize the values or, as the *Ratio* says, to "act more from inner principles." One begins thinking like a monk. Usually you like to see this happening before solemn vows, but it does not stop there. The process goes on for years and years. In fact, we are in formation throughout our monastic life. The final stage of formation is the longest. It is described in the prayer I began with—living not by our own strength but by the strength of another. I think this is the inner meaning of our vows, especially our vow of obedience. It is a vow made to God to be obedient to his word and to live his will.

I found two major points in the readings for our Advent liturgy that speak of this type of formation. The first comes from the prophecy of Isaiah: "Your ears will hear these words behind you. This is the way; keep to it" (Isa 30). This reminds me of the

phrase, "A voice I did not know said to me." This is guidance
and direction coming from a source outside us. It does not come
from our own discernment; it comes from trusting the voice of
God. This calls for surrender on our part, and a deep trust.

The other point stems from a global impression we are given
in all the Gospels during the first week of Advent. In the readings
Jesus is shown spending most of his time with the downtrodden,
the marginalized, the weak, the infirm, people who suffered, the
dispossessed, and the little people of no account. This is an image
of who we are as monks, persons whose egos are diminished. It
is a painful process, but we do take a vow of poverty, a vow of
obedience. We are called to surrender ourselves, hand ourselves
over, to be possessed by another, by God.

This process of dispossession really goes on in everyone's
life sooner or later. As we approach old age and illness, we can
do less and less for ourselves. Our faculties are gradually diminished until death overtakes us. In this sense, our monastic life is
an anticipation of death. We give up our very selves that we may
be possessed by God. Our weaknesses are what attract God. St.
Paul said, "When I am weak, then I am strong" (2 Cor 12:10). By
willingly embracing our human condition, our weaknesses of
body and soul, we are preparing ourselves for the visitation of
the Lord.

Our daily life in community gives us many opportunities to
be dispossessed, to give up our control over things, to become
one of the little ones, the *anawim*, the poor of Yahweh. The steps
of humility are meant to empty us of all that is not God so that
by the time we reach the twelfth degree of humility, we will have
become totally surrendered. We will have become transparent
bearers of the Holy Spirit, living not by our own strength but
from God.

When we begin living from inner principles and the strength
of another, then we realize this ability comes from our prayer
life. In the monastery, it is not important that we try to figure out
what stage of prayer we may have reached. We are not looking
for the extraordinary graces of prayer the great mystics wrote

about, but there is a progression in our prayer lives, just as there is in our awareness of who we are as monks. One of the marks of our growth in prayer is the desire to surrender ourselves to God, to Jesus, to the Spirit, to be possessed by God totally. This type of transformation in prayer can come about very quietly, very slowly, and calmly. Often we may not even be aware it is happening. We find ourselves making interior acts of abandonment to God, acts or prayers of surrender, of handing over our very selves to God.

St. John of the Cross says, "In the transformation of love each gives possession of self for the other. Thus each one lives in the other and is the other and both are one in the transformation of love." He concludes, "This is the meaning of Paul's affirmation, 'I live now not I but Christ lives in me'" (Gal 2:20).[73] If we desire the inner transformation of our prayer, we have to live this way of surrender in our daily life, to be dispossessed and possessed in our spirit. We must go through the same transformation in our behavior. We cannot have one without the other.

St. Bernard speaks of being penetrated in the depths of his being by the visitation of the Word. He says, "The Bridegroom-Word, though He has several times entered into me, had never made His coming apparent to my sight, hearing or touch. . . . It was only by the revived activity of my heart that I was enabled to recognize His presence. . . . " Then he uses a very down-to-earth image to describe the withdrawal of the Presence. He says, "But when the Word withdrew Himself, all these spiritual powers and faculties began to droop and languish, as if the fire had been withdrawn from a bubbling pot, and this is to me the sign of His departure" (Sermon 74:6-7 on the Canticle of Canticles). We know how quickly boiling water stops bubbling when we turn off the stove. But St. Bernard says it is at this time that truth must be served, even when the grace may not be apparent; we still must live the truth and put into practice the teaching of the Scriptures.

---

73. St. John of the Cross, *Spiritual Canticle*, stanza 12:6-7, *The Collected Works of John of the Cross* (Washington, DC: ICS Publications, 1973).

Quest for Union with God

We read in John 3:16 that God so loved the world he gave his only Son, that through him we might have eternal life. Christ was sent to save the world. Then in other passages, we find different symbols for Jesus, such as the light of the world (John 8:12) or the bread of life (John 6:35). He is this image of the unseen God, the firstborn of all creation. He existed before all, and in him all fullness is to be found (Col 1:15-17).

These last acclamations are used as the basis of the argument that Christ would have come into the world even if there was no original sin. In other words, redemption does not express the complete ministry of Christ. Certainly Christ came to redeem us, but he also came that we might have union with him.

The ancient monks saw the monastic life as a return to paradise, a place of union. They believed that a life of asceticism, especially prayer, would lead to our original state of being. Buried deep in the heart of each person is a true self that emerges in prayer, in silence and solitude. Asceticism brings an inner freedom to the monk. Seen in this light, the penance practiced and handed down to us by the early monks has a very positive meaning. It is a means to greater inner freedom, a way of allowing our true self to emerge.

This concept of a true self is common to many religions. The experience of the self according to Hinduism is the highest attainment a person can achieve. For us it is the point where the Holy Spirit and the self become one, the union restored for us in Christ. It is the reconciliation of all things in Christ that St. Paul talks about in the hymn in Colossians (Col 1:20).

St. John of the Cross speaks of the soul having many centers but only one deepest center. This is the place of its purest and most intimate awareness, the central point of the self. Here is where the gift of wisdom begins to grow. The wisdom which the early monks sought was not a worldly wisdom but a spiritual wisdom, and they put all their efforts into acquiring it. The gift of wisdom makes us experience the fact that by grace we are partakers of the divine nature. St. Thomas Aquinas says that we have a connaturality with God. To experience this connaturality is what the experience of the self is for monks. It is the self in its truest form, not isolated and alone but united and born in God. Prayer is the language of the union.

St. John Chrysostom says, "Prayer and converse with God is a supreme good: it is a partnership and union with God." Since he wrote in Greek, I suppose he would have used *koinonia* for the word "partnership." *Koinonia*, the Greek word for community, fellowship, or partnership with God, is the basis of our community life, our common life. He goes on, "As the eyes of the body are enlightened when they see light, so our spirit, when it is intent on God, is illumined by his infinite light." Many of the Fathers use this image of the light of God shining in our spirits. It is an inner light, the natural environment of our soul. The mystery of Christ's Transfiguration revealed and made known this life, manifested what we ordinarily cannot see. At the moment of death we will see it, or at a moment of prayer we might experience it.

St. John Chrysostom goes on to explain what type of prayer brings us to this place of light, this place of our true spirit. He says, "I do not mean the prayer of outward observance but prayer from the heart, not confined to fixed times or periods but continuous throughout the day and night."[74]

This is the classic teaching of the early monks about continuous prayer. It means to continually be intent on God. This is the reason for their extreme teaching on silence and solitude. The Desert Fathers summed up their teachings in Latin: *fuge, tace, quiesce* (flee, be still, and be quiet). This was to allow space for God. Thomas Merton claims that this word *quies*, or "rest" is what we would call contemplative prayer today. The Greeks called it *hesychia* (repose). Merton says that it is a silent absorption aided by the soft repetition of a lone phrase of Scripture.[75]

---

74. Taken from the Breviary, Office of Readings, Friday after Ash Wednesday.
75. Thomas Merton, *Wisdom of the Desert: Sayings from the Desert Fathers of the Fourth Century* (New York: New Directions, 1961), 20.

Vacate et Videte (Be empty and see), or as another translator has it, "be still and know." This is the motto on our monastery coat of arms. Be empty that you may be filled with the fullness of life. The journey to this place of stillness is very difficult, and we can easily lose our way. The monastic life, including its observances and customs, is meant to keep us on the road. It is a radical way of living, and there is danger involved because we can separate the goal from the means to attain the goal. Then all we have is observances and customs with no heart. Cassian is very clear about keeping on the path. Like an arrow on its way to the target, we should not veer to the left or the right. The goal is purity of heart, *quies, hesychia*, the place of light, or the experience of the self before God and in God.

We have to be careful not to lose sight of the goal. Otherwise coming to the monastery will be nothing more than leaving one society, that of the world, to fit ourselves into another kind of society, that of our religious family. It is possible to exchange the values, concepts, and rites of the one for those of the other, and as Merton says, "the social norms of our monasteries are apt to be conventional and to live by them does not involve a leap into the void, only a radical change of customs and standards."[76]

While we focus on the truth of our monastic vocation at all times, Lent is the appropriate time for going deeper. St. Benedict speaks of it as a time of prayer with tears, the prayer of compunction that pierces our hearts and opens us to the grace of our real vocation of union with God through the monastic way, the conversation of our daily life. Underneath it all is that silent stream flowing, the river of God's love in our life, the fullness of life that Jesus means to give us.

Presence and Recognition of Christ

On the feast of the Presentation of the Lord (February 2), there are two things we are all familiar with and take for granted,

76. Ibid., 10.

namely, presence and recognition. We recognize each other's presence, our physical presence and our emotional presence. We even speak of someone having an imposing presence or an air of authority. This feast invites us to a deeper experience of presence. It is the presence which only faith can recognize, the presence of the Divine in the human. The feast recounts the presentation of Jesus in the temple.

On the level of what our eyes can see, Jesus was an ordinary Jewish child, an ordinary Jewish man who died a criminal's death. But to the eyes of faith, we see the mystery of the Divine in the human.

The candles we received and held in our hands at this morning's liturgy represent the light of faith, the illumination of our eyes, the recognition faith brings to our life. Things are not as they appear. Recognition and appearance are not the same. Appearances are deceiving. We all know this, but it is still a wonder when we are surprised by the beauty of the Divine in the human.

Several years ago a group of high school students came here on retreat. We usually do not encourage high school retreats because students that age tend to be noisy and restless. About three days is their limit. This group was true to form. By the third morning I could tell they wanted to get out of here. To look at them, they looked like any other group of teenagers—to be honest, they looked like they did not have a thought in their heads. But appearance is deceiving. I asked them to write down a paragraph or two about their retreat experiences, and I was astounded at the depth of what they revealed. One boy wrote:

> My monastic experience has been one I never will forget. I
> very recently lost an old friend of mine in a motorcycle ac-
> cident. On the way down here my emotions ranged from
> joy and excitement to sadness and depression. When we
> arrived, I feared the silence because I had nothing from
> keeping me from thinking of my friend's death. When we
> went into the chapel for the first time for Compline, I sat
> there afterwards and cried silently for my friend. Then, as
> God always seems to do for me, I saw the candle over the

tabernacle and was awestruck. The symbolism of that lone flickering light was amazing. I suddenly thought that each one of us has one of these lights inside of them, the candle symbolizing our soul. This light is blown about by sin and temptation and strengthened by faith in God and good works. This light, like the candle, will burn always in the hearts and minds of others. This comforted me because it helped me come to the realization that even though my friend is dead, he will never die as long as the people who loved him remember him.

"He will never die as long as the people who loved him remember him." At this Eucharist we are the ones who love Jesus and remember him. Our remembrance brings his presence to us. It is what we call the "Real Presence."

Appearances are deceiving. The bread and wine are the Body and Blood of Christ. The Body and Blood are the love Christ has for the Father and for us. They are handed over and poured out for us and our salvation.

Jesus Living through Us

A dictionary-size book on the complete works of St. Louis de Montfort is not entitled *The Collected Works of St. Louis de Montfort*, but rather *Jesus Living through Mary*. The phrase possibly comes from his writings.

Jesus Living through Mary. This expression signifies the relationship of our devotions to the Sacred Heart of Jesus and the Immaculate Heart of Mary. The title of the book I just mentioned gives one a better understanding of the profound devotion of St. Louis to Mary. For him, Jesus comes and touches his soul through Mary. She is in a certain sense a female form of Jesus. Someone who has the grace of this devotion does not have to make a mental leap from Mary to Jesus. There is a perceived unity of the hearts. One is in the other. After all, does not St. Paul say this about every Christian baptized into Christ? They are "in" Christ. Paul uses prepositions quite frequently to express our relationship with Christ in various ways. He speaks of "in" Christ, also "with" Christ, and "through" Christ.

St. Benedict does something similar in the twelfth degree of humility. The main characteristic of the twelfth degree is love. We no longer act out of fear but out of love for Christ. Benedict ends the chapter with the words, "the Lord will graciously make all this *shine forth* in the monk by the power of the Holy Spirit." Another translation reads, "All this the Lord will *show forth* by the Holy Spirit in his servant now cleansed from vice and sin." The steps of humility are shown as a dynamic process leading to a transformation of our lives, our consciousness, our very awareness of who we are, our identity. Once purified, we become channels or bearers of the Holy Spirit. All the translations use the words "shine forth," "show forth," or "manifest." What, exactly, is manifested in the complete monk or the purified monk if not the life of Christ? The love of Christ will be so strong that the monastic will become an instrument of the Holy Spirit.

We can imagine adding our own names to the title of de Montfort's book: "Jesus living through Raymond or Daniel or Br. Augustine, or each one of us." Or it could be "Jesus sharing his suffering in Br. Benedict."

Our Constitutions speak of our life as having a hidden fruitfulness in the Church. Our union with Christ or Christ living in us is the source of this fruitfulness. It might be good to reflect on our place in the hidden fruitfulness of the Church. If we look at our mission in the Church, the word "hidden" is very important. Something hidden can easily be forgotten. When we forget who we are and what our mission is, then we can easily see the monastery as a place of self-maintenance, a self-improvement project, rather than a mission in the Church. In the monastic life, who we are and our mission are one and the same.

I was reminded of this recently at Mass on the feast of the Sacred Heart. The preface for a feast day is usually a very concise statement of what the feast is all about, in this case, "From His wounded side flowed blood and water, the fountain of sacramental life in the Church. To His open heart the Savior invites all people to draw water in joy for the springs of salvation."

The understanding here is that the sacramental life of the Church is the visible life, and the sacraments are just those visible signs which have an invisible source symbolized by the pierced heart of Jesus from which flowed blood and water. In other words, the heart of Jesus, or the love of Jesus, is the source of the visible life of the Church. We are called to live at this point of love. In a real way, our life becomes sacramental, both interiorly and exteriorly, a visible life of monastic observances coming from an invisible source within us.

There is a long history of interiority in the contemplative life. We are often told to enter into ourselves, to find the place of our heart, even to experience the vast emptiness of our being. It is to experience not so much what we are, but *that* we are. Dom Bernardo, our Abbot General, described modern mysticism as an apprehension of one's interiority, the experience of deep presence and communion from within one's own depths.

The word used to describe this place of presence and communion is "heart." The word used to describe the communion is "prayer." Prayer is a union of hearts. It can even be an exchange of hearts. Kallistos Ware says:

> When we pray you yourself must be silent. Let the prayer speak. To achieve silence this is of all things the hardest and most decisive in the art of prayer. Silence is an attitude of attentive alertness, of vigilance and above all of listening. The hesychist, the one who has attained *hesychia*, inward stillness or silence, is par excellence the one who listens. He listens to the voice of prayer in his own heart and understands that the voice is not his own but that of another speaking within him.[77]

This is the voice of Jesus who is always praying to the Father. In the preface of the Sacred Heart, this is called the fountain of sacramental life, and a little later, a spring of water. These are beautiful symbols of the prayer of Jesus always flowing within us.

---

77. Kallistos Ware, *The Power of the Name* (Oxford: Fairacres Press, 1979), 3.

Let me conclude this reflection with a paragraph from the Dominican mystic John Tauler. He writes:

> [when a person] recollects himself and enters into the temple [the inner self] in which . . . he finds God dwelling and at work, [he] then comes to experience God not after the fashion of the senses and of reason, or like something that one understands or reads . . . but he tastes Him and enjoys Him like something that springs up from the "ground" of the soul as from its own source, or from a fountain, without having been brought there, for a fountain is better than a cistern, the water of cisterns gets stale and evaporates, but the spring flows, bursts out, swells: it is true, not borrowed. It is sweet.[78]

INSPIRATIONS FROM THE LIFE OF MARY

Christ's Redemptive Grace and Immaculate Conception

On December 8, 1854, Pope Pius IX proclaimed the dogma of the Immaculate Conception as an article of faith. His pronouncement settled a dispute among theologians known as the "Maculists" and the "Immaculists." The Maculists, following St. Thomas Aquinas and St. Bernard, taught that Mary, at her conception, first incurred original sin and then received fullness of grace. The Immaculists, following John Duns Scotus, taught that Christ's merits were applied to Mary in advance so that she was never separated from God by sin even for an instant. To their (the Immaculists') minds this displayed the power of Christ as Mediator in a more perfect way.

The decree of Pius IX, *Ineffabilis Deus*, put an end to the dispute. The Pope chose the Immaculist position. Ever since then we have summarized the dogma by saying that Mary was pre-

78. Quotation on the mystic John Tauler by Thomas Merton, *The Inner Experience*, ibid. 13.

served from sin from the moment of her conception. We have left it at that and gone our way. The dogma of the Immaculate Conception has thus become remote from everyday life and poorly understood. If all we can say about it is that Mary was preserved from sin, then how are we to respond?

Nowadays we want to know what is in it for us. Or, put in a more sophisticated manner, the dogmas of the Church are teachings that reveal divine life and illumine our life. How does the dogma of the Immaculate Conception illumine our life? To say that Mary was preserved from sin does not appeal to modern people. We don't especially like exemptions, or maybe we want them for ourselves but not for others. We want an even playing field—no special favors. Traditional lives of saints that begin with "he was of noble birth" or "her mother was granted a vision before her birth" leave us cold. We tend to be more like Joseph's brothers, whose reaction to his dream was, "who do you think you are, putting yourself above us?" This way of thinking is understandable and common, but it is mean-spirited all the same. Maybe what the hagiographers were trying to tell us is that the saint was not noble by his blood line as much as by his spirit. He was capable of noble thoughts and actions.

We have to raise ourselves to a higher and nobler way of thinking to appreciate the Immaculate Conception—to appreciate someone receiving a special favor. We have to broaden our horizons to take in the whole human race as a family and Mary as the new Eve, the mother of all the living. A privilege given to her is an honor for all in the family. The privilege is not only freedom from sin, but the other side of that is her holiness. She is called the "All Holy,"*Panagia* in the Eastern Church, "full of grace" in the Western Church.

It can all get very confusing when we say Mary, who was born before Christ, was the first to receive the grace of his Resurrection, or as Edward Schillebeeckx puts it, "on the Cross Mary was at the center of Christ's being"—but she was also standing under the cross. These statements sound confusing because we are trying to express divine realities in human words.

The basic line is that God's love for Mary penetrated so deeply that at the very moment of her conception, right at the seed of her life, God was with her. This does not mean that she was freed from suffering; it means that her life conformed perfectly to the life of her Son, and in this, she is our model. We too are called to a Marian devotion to Christ: to conform our lives as perfectly as we can to the pattern of his Passion, Death, and Resurrection.

This is how the feast of the Immaculate Conception is meant to illumine our life: the healing presence of Christ, which we call grace, is meant to penetrate back into our history and with the water of baptism cleanse us from the very moment our body and soul are made one. Christ's redeeming grace restores what was lost through sin and makes whole what was shattered.

Mother of All Living by Faith

When the deacon read the Gospel yesterday for the Second Sunday of Advent, I couldn't help contrasting it with the Gospel for the Solemnity of the Immaculate Conception. Both are stories of the Word of God coming to individuals—John the Baptist and Mary. Both have a mission. But how different they are! John the Baptist almost becomes violent. He thunders forth as a voice crying in the wilderness. He calls those presenting themselves for baptism a "brood of vipers"! It's not a very warm welcome! There are other instances of this type in the Bible. God comes to Moses in a tremendous storm, so terrible that the people don't dare go near the mountain. In Mark's Gospel Jesus is not *led* into the desert, he is *driven* there by the Holy Spirit. The coming of the Word of God causes a violent upheaval—something dramatic takes place, and life does not go on as usual. Our only response is a radical demand to change.

But there is another type of divine visitation. It is quiet as a whispering wind, gentle as an angel approaching a maiden, as in Luke's description of the Annunciation (Luke 1:26-38). Listen to how the Word came to Mary: "The Holy Spirit will come upon you and the power of the Most High will cover you with its shadow"

(Luke 1:35). There are no thunderclaps or cosmic upheavals here. The power of God is as soothing as the wings of a dove, a cooling shadow cast by the bright cloud of God's presence. Jesus is conceived in this tender moment when the Holy Spirit comes upon Mary and the power of the Most High covers her in its shade.

The feast of the Immaculate Conception flows from the Gospel about the Annunciation. The angel declares Mary full of grace. We interpret that to mean not just at the moment of speaking but from the moment of her conception. Full of grace, she is what the Eastern Fathers call "all holy" (*pan-agia*, completely holy). We apply the words of Paul's letter to the Ephesians to Mary: "Chosen in Christ before the world was made to be holy and spotless before him in love" (Eph 1:4). "How can this be?" are the exact words of Mary, and we hear them several times in the Gospels. "How can this be?" I don't understand. But this did not stop her. Not to understand and yet consent is the example Mary gives us. It is what faith is all about. Eve is called the "mother of those who live" (Gen 3:20). Mary is the mother of those who live by faith. The mysteries of her life, from her Immaculate Conception to her Assumption, are like a many-faceted diamond reflecting Jesus to us. Let us look deeply into this diamond. At once we will see her prerogatives as the *Theotokos*, the Mother of God. Then again we see her as the Sorrowful Mother. Look again and we see her not understanding, saying, "How can this be?" We can go there, we can identify with this question, and yet we do not stop there. Like Mary, we give our consent and believe in order to understand.

And so the Word comes to us as it did two thousand years ago to Mary. Her silence speaks louder than the thundering voice of John the Baptist. The favor of God rests upon her like a shadow, a cool shade in the hot desert, for she is "earth's sweetness at its beginning" (Gerard Manley Hopkins).

Spending the Fullness of Time with Mary

Time. What is time? Stephen Hawking wrote a book entitled *A Brief History of Time*. St. Augustine said he knows what time is until he tries to define it. In ordinary speech we use the word loosely. We talk about daytime and nighttime, long time, short time, historical time, psychological time, physiological time, past time, present time, future time, but we never use the words "the completion of time" or "the fullness of time." This is how Paul sees time in Galatians 4:4: "When the fullness of time came." We don't think in terms of the completion of time. Yet, this is the revelation. We are living in the fullness of time, the completion of time. This does not mean time is over, it means time is full, nothing is lacking. God sending his son, born of a woman, into the world marks the fullness of time.

Each year we celebrate that woman, Mary, as the Mother of God. It is done on the first day of the secular year which we call the New Year. By celebrating her feast as the year begins, we entrust it to her, we pray that the coming year will be under her protection, her care. We can even say we will spend the time with Mary.

There are many important things we don't know about the days, weeks, and months that are coming when the new year begins. First of all, we don't know if we will even be here when it ends! Secondly, if we are here, we don't know what our health of mind and body will be. These are important considerations, but they are not the most crucial. What is much more important is that right now and all throughout the coming year, for however much time we have, we will live in the fullness of time—the completion of time.

Spending time with Mary can lead us to the fullness of time. Here is how St. Ambrose puts it: "Let Mary's soul be in each of you . . ." What is Mary's soul? It is her most profound being—the place of her greatest transparency before God. It is where God comes to her. The Father overshadows her. It is where the Holy Spirit becomes her spouse and the Word becomes flesh as Jesus. It is where she becomes the Mother of God. It is where the fullness of time begins. And we are there. If we let Mary's soul live in us, we will live in the fullness of time.

"Let Mary's soul be in each of you to proclaim the greatness of God." When we do this in prayer, in the Divine Office, and in the way we live, we are in the fullness of time. St. Ambrose goes even further. He says when we believe, we conceive and bring forth the Word of God.

Each day of the year will demand many things of us—maybe even our lives. It will call for many acts of faith. Mary is called blessed because she believed. Our lives will be truly blessed if we believe and let Mary's soul live in us.

Mary's Yes to God Planted in the Heart of Her Child

I know people who cannot stand the suspense of a mystery novel so they read the last chapter first. Having discovered the ending they turn back and start at the beginning. I wonder, has there ever been a person who has read the Gospel accounts of Jesus' life without knowing the ending? I suspect most of us knew the ending by the time we were in the first grade, if not earlier. What would it be like to follow Jesus through the Gospels, chapter by chapter, without knowing beforehand how the story was going to end? Would we not be in the position of the first disciples who walked with Jesus? They were kept in suspense at least until Jesus rose from the dead. Once the Resurrection took place and they regrouped around the one they abandoned on Calvary, they were taught to reread the Scriptures. In fact, Jesus taught them two very important things, and we can reflect on both of them today as we celebrate the feast of the Annunciation.

First, Jesus made sure his disciples knew he had a body. He was not a ghost. He was flesh and blood. He made it a point to eat with them and show them the wounds in his hands and feet. He would bring this body and these wounds into heaven with him. This is the same body Mary gave him from her womb. Flesh from her flesh, blood from her blood. This is the same flesh and blood Jesus offered to the Father on the cross. The same flesh and blood we offer and receive at each Eucharist, only now it is glorified flesh and blood, not bound by physical limitations. It even appears under the form of bread and wine. So we see a wonderful unity in the body, from Mary to Jesus to each of us. This makes

Mary our Mother through the body and blood of Christ. We share the same body. St. Leo says it beautifully, "As the Word does not lose equality with the Father's glory, so the flesh does not leave behind the nature of our race."[79]

The other thing Jesus taught his disciples was how to read the Scriptures. He did this by showing them the places in Scripture that applied to him. The Church, especially in her liturgy, still does this. Today she has chosen readings from Isaiah and Hebrews and applied them to Mary. She is the Virgin whom Isaiah spoke of centuries ago. She is intimately a part of the theology of worship spelled out in the epistle to the Hebrews: "this will was for us to be made holy by the offering of the body of Jesus Christ made once and for all" (Heb 10:10). Jesus made very sure his disciples knew he had a real body after the Resurrection. A true body carried into eternity—a true glorified body being offered to the Father in an outpouring of love every day in the Eucharist.

When we celebrate Mary's acceptance of her role in the plan of salvation at the Annunciation, we recognize that it was she who prepared the way for God to enter our lives as man. A man coming to do God's will. Can we not say that Mary not only gave the man Jesus his body but she also taught the child how to do God's will? She who accepted in faith the Will of God into her heart planted the seed in the heart of her child that grew into a complete and total dedication to the will of the Father.

Mary's Assumption: After-Death, Key to Life

One day as I was celebrating weekday Mass I saw a woman arrive a little late. I remembered she had lost her adult son several months earlier. It happened on the same day that the forty-one-year-old son of one of our lay workers was being buried. A week before that, we had a note from a friend asking prayers for her eighteen-year-old son who had been killed in an auto accident. It is one thing for a ninety-three-year-old monk to die, but how

---

79. St. Leo the Great, taken from the Liturgy of the Hours, March 25.

do you deal with the death of a child or young adult? We all search for answers to questions like this. We can try to avoid thinking about death, but sometimes it thrusts itself into our life unexpectedly and we are forced to deal with it.

Every religion has to have answers to this ultimate question. It's not so much why do we have to die, but rather, what happens after death? I always marvel at how quickly we deal with death in the monastery. A monk dies, and a few days later he is buried, and a few weeks later he is almost forgotten. We have a remarkable ability to keep death at a distance—unless it is the death of a parent or a child or a loved one. Then it is forced upon us with an urgency we can hardly stand. Think of the two disciples on their way to Emmaus. When Jesus died they thought it was all over. All their dreams came crashing down. They had thought there was more to it than that. They had assumed that Jesus would restore Israel, make their life better, and free them from the Romans. Jesus did free them, but not from the Romans. Jesus freed them from death itself. He gave us all the answer to death by rising from the dead. He didn't just talk about life after death; he showed us life after death. He is the answer to the ultimate puzzle of life.

The Gospels were written in light of the Resurrection. We have to look at the events in our own lives from the same vantage point. There is no real end to our life. True, death is some kind of an end, but it is more than that; it is a beginning.

The feast of Mary's Assumption is about what happens after death. It is also a key to what is happening in our lives. If you look at Mary's life as recorded in the Gospels there is nothing special about it. It is a life of faith, not vision. It is only divine revelation that lets us look at the hidden glory of her life. Revelation tells us that at her death, or dormition, she was assumed body and soul into heaven, the first one of our race to share in the Resurrection of Jesus. She is the first to have a glorified body. When we bury someone, we leave the body in the grave believing that on the last day it will rise in glory. Mary is already enjoying that union with her body and her Son. From the vantage point of her Assumption we can look back on all the mysteries of her life and see the full meaning of her faith.

Because of Christ's Resurrection and Mary's Assumption we have hope that our death is a beginning but also that in our life we can look back from that vantage point and find the infinite in the finite. There is so much more going on in our life than we can see or understand or even imagine. When Mary conceived Jesus in her womb she had a life within her life. Every woman who has conceived must have experienced this—a life within her life. This seems to me to be a model for all Christians. We have a life within our life. We have the life of God within our life. We have to be attentive to the life we bear, nurture it and bring forth its fruit. Nothing is as it seems. Death is life, suffering is redemptive, and mortality becomes immortality.

St. Therese is called the saint of the little way, the ordinary way, the nothing special way. One of her biographers says, "The uniqueness of Therese's message does not lie in what she confided to her loved ones, but in the fact that she dared to express it at all. Because of this, countless persons realize that this existence of theirs is a 'way,' even a way of sanctity."[80]

Each of us has a *way*, a life to be lived. It may not be dramatic, but it is a revelation of God's love to us. When St. Benedict died, two monks saw a magnificent road covered with rich carpeting and glittering with thousands of lights. From the monastery it stretched eastward in a straight line until it reached up into heaven. There in the brightness stood a man who told the monks that this was the road taken by Blessed Benedict. We all have a road to travel, a way. It may seem ordinary but, hopefully, it leads to heaven, and someday we may be able to look back and see how bright and beautiful the road really was.

80. Ida Gorres, biographer of St. Therese of Lisieux.

Queen and Mother of Mercy

One of the important titles of Mary is "Mother of Mercy." As I reflect on these words it reminds me of the role of Marian devotion in our Cistercian life. It is part of our patrimony, coming to us more from St. Bernard than from St. Benedict or the Desert Fathers.

Every evening when we sing the *Salve Regina* we pray that Mary will turn her eyes of mercy towards us. We all know what brown eyes or blue eyes look like. But what do the eyes of mercy look like? The eyes are said to be windows to the soul. St. Bernard calls Mary a pool of grace. Her eyes of mercy lead us into the realm of grace, the place of mercy.

Usually we think of the eyes as receptors. The eyes take in what they see. But eyes also present. They give a look. The way we look at people tells them how we are feeling towards them. We have all received a hostile look at one time or another, and we know what a lustful look is. In fact, looks are so powerful that our Lord tells us they can cause us to sin in our hearts (Matt 5:28). A look can convey a whole range of expressions and feelings. There is a look of hate, a look of boredom, a look of joy, then a look of tenderness, of love, of mercy.

It is important how we look at each other. The word "look" is often expanded to mean our general stance toward something or someone. We often say, I look at the situation like this . . . I see it differently . . . I look at him and think . . .

It is important that we look at each other with eyes of mercy. There is an interesting section in the readings from St. Augustine's sermons on pastors. He says, "For what man can judge rightly concerning another? Our whole daily life is filled with rash judgments. He of whom we had despaired is converted suddenly and becomes very good. He from whom we had anticipated a great deal suddenly fails and becomes very bad. Neither our fear nor our hope is certain. What any man is today, that man himself scarcely knows."[81]

---

81. St. Augustine, taken from the Liturgy of the Hours, Friday of the Twenty-Fifth Week of the Year.

Mercy can short-circuit our usual path to rash judgment. A look of mercy can mean that our predominant approach to life, to others, and to ourselves is mercy. If we start with that we will not go astray. St. Bernard teaches this as the beginning of self-knowledge. When we realize our own sinfulness and forgiveness, we then extend that inner experience to others. We know the mercy of God and therefore we express it to others.

St. Bernard reminds us that Mary is the star that guides us in our sea. Whatever currents are moving in our sea, Mary is there to guide and lead us. In this instance, she is the Mother of Mercy showing us how to be merciful.

A mother creates a nurturing place for her child, a secure place where the child feels safe and can learn how to trust and love. Without this place, a child's life becomes chaos and he or she becomes distrustful and cautious, suspicious and guarded. There is no spontaneity in an insecure place. A mother by her love creates safe places for her child. You could even call them sacred places.

Mary has created several such places for us. Think of them. We see Mary pondering Jesus at his birth in the stable at Bethlehem, pondering in her heart when she and Joseph found him in the temple, standing outside waiting for him, and above all, standing at the foot of the cross. These are sacred and safe places for us to be in spirit. These places become a home for us, dwelling places for our spirits. They are the temple of worship where we can silently adore and love God in prayer. If we journey through the Gospels with Mary, we find many sacred places for contemplation, places that open the heavens as it was opened for St. Stephen. "Look," he exclaimed, "I see an opening in the sky and the Son of Man standing at God's right hand" (Acts 7:56).

We all search for that opening in the sky. Mary in fact is called the door, the portal, the gate of heaven. Through her we have access to the mystery where she stood with Jesus, those sacred places of prayer. In the Gospels, her words are few, but she is there pondering in her heart what her eyes take in.

One of the psalms that we read on Saturday is Psalm 86:5 (87:5). It is often used in conjunction with Mary, especially the words, "and Zion shall be called mother, for all shall be her children. It is he the Lord Most High who gives each his place." As Cistercians we claim a special place in those sacred places where Mary ponders the mystery of her Son in the Gospels. The psalm concludes with the words, "In you all find their home" (86:7).

Mary is a home, not just a house but a home of security, trust, peace, love, and mercy. This is what we want our home here in the monastery to be. This kind of a home is vital to our life. We will suffocate in a community where there is no love, where we cannot live in peace, where there is no trust and security, where there is no mercy. We need to receive it and to give it. Mercy has many dimensions, and it is expressed through forgiveness, respect, humility, strength of character, peace, patience, kindness, and compassion.

I see mercy as an attribute of the senior monks. St. Bernard identified it correctly when he said that compassion and mercy flow from a heart that has been pierced by its own weakness and suffering. We have to be compassionate to ourselves before we can be compassionate and merciful to others. Many of us have an accusing and judging voice playing in our heads all the time. If we are not vigilant, those two traits will become the predominant way we look at our brothers.

On September 25, we celebrate the votive Mass honoring Mary as Queen and Mother of Mercy. These are the first words of the *Salve Regina*: "Hail, Holy Queen, Mother of Mercy, hail, our life, our sweetness and our hope!" I love the way the poet Gerard Manley Hopkins speaks of her: "Mary is earth's sweetness at its beginning." There is sweetness in life, a core of joy and happiness, but it is easily overlooked in all the trials of life. We do acknowledge this fact in the *Salve*. We are singing this song from a vale of tears, pleading for eyes of mercy to turn toward us.

"O Clement, O loving, O sweet Virgin Mary!" These are the words with which we close our day. Maria is the last official word of the monastery. After it, the great silence begins. During a singing class at Our Lady of Atlas Monastery, one of the cantors said that the last word of the *Salve* is meant to be a shout, not a sigh. I must admit, however, that by the time I get to the end of that hymn I barely have enough breath left to whisper let alone to shout, "O Clement, O loving, O sweet Virgin Mary." Virgin Mary comes out like a sigh. But what can you do? Mary understands.

The Many Faces of Mary

January is named after the Roman god Janus, who is depicted with two faces, as if he is looking back to the past with one face and ahead into the future with the other. If we think of the year as a circle, January 1 is the point where the circle ends and begins, and as such the yearly cycle is a symbol of eternity.

The idea of someone having two faces is not too far-fetched. We know what it means to be called "two faced." In fact, we have more than two faces; we have many faces. We have a happy face, a sad face, an anxious face, an angry face. Once I received an e-mail from the secretary of another monastery's abbot. He broke off the letter with the words, "I have to go now; the abbot just came in wearing his angry face!"

On January 1, the beginning and the ending of the year, we celebrate the feast of Mary as Mother of God. We could say that this feast includes all of Mary's titles. We might call it "the feast of the many faces of Mary," and if we search the Gospels we can find them. At the Annunciation she shows a concerned questioning face; at the visitation, a joyful, ecstatic face; at the birth of Jesus, a contemplative, wonder-struck face; the finding in the temple reveals an anxious, worried face; and at the foot of the cross, a sorrowful, suffering face. We can identify with all of these faces, and we can even have a favorite one that draws us into the mystery of Mary.

The face reveals what is going on in a person's heart. In Luke's Gospel Simeon prophesies that Mary's heart will be pierced with a sword, and the thoughts of many hearts will be revealed (Luke 2:16-21). How does the piercing of Mary's heart reveal the thoughts of many hearts? Thoughts are hidden, especially the deep thoughts of the heart. I take the piercing of the heart to be hidden also. Mary is the first of the redeemed to journey through life. Every human experience she had, every face she shows us, has a human and a spiritual dimension. She is the first Christian and as such is a model for all others. We were redeemed at baptism but still must live our lives in such a way as to strengthen the graces of baptism.

The liturgy and popular devotion have given Mary many names. None is sweeter than "mother," *Theotokos*, the Mother of God. This truly is a mystery beyond us, but we can all identify with the title "mother." Mary acts on our behalf like a loving mother to her child. Mary is most approachable with her motherly face. Popular devotion has given Mary many other names, and we will encounter them as we journey through this coming year to arrive at next January. This encounter will reveal the thoughts of our hearts, and it will reveal who we really are. Mary is called "Health of the Sick," "Refuge of Sinners," and "Comfort of the Afflicted." Each of these has a face we are familiar with because they are ours. No doubt, some of us will be sick in the coming year, perhaps seriously ill; all of us will be tempted to sin, and face some kind of affliction. How we deal with these sufferings reveals who we are. The thoughts of the heart show on the face of a sick person. Mary is deeply involved with our cause. She is the health of the sick soul, the refuge of the failed soul, the comfort of the afflicted soul. You see, we face life on two levels, the physical and the spiritual. Mary is present to us on the soul level. Her face reflects the suffering of all of us. She has been there and knows from experience how everything leads to her Son, Jesus.

The face we see in the Gospel at the presentation is a contemplative face. The Gospel says Mary pondered in her heart, or treasured, which means to hold close to the heart. We treasure life's great moments. We ponder what is not self-evident, and we want to go deeper in our understanding of the mystery of the soul. How can we best describe Mary's contemplative face? Here, poetic words work best. One title above all others speaks to us of the depths of her heart. She is known as the "Mystical Rose." The rose is the cherished symbol of love. Love and suffering. The dark center of the rose is inaccessible; to get there you would have to destroy the rose. The rose must be intuited, not analyzed. A mystical rose is one of a kind, unique on the earth. Just so is Mary. We come to know Mary more through intuition than analysis, more through prayer than study. The thoughts of her heart are beyond us but not foreign to us. She is the swan, we are the paddlers, but we are in the same lake learning from her.

As we circle the sun this year we will meet the many faces of Mary. Underneath the face is the heart, the mystical heart of Mary revealing the mystery of her Son present in our life. The many faces we wear through the year, the many experiences we will have, the many thoughts of our heart can only be fully known in prayer. Like Mary we must treasure all these things in our hearts. There the mystical rose grows as in a garden of the soul.

Call on Mary, She Forms Our Hearts

On the feast of Our Lady of Guadalupe (December 12), Fr. Xavier read a beautiful passage from St. Bernard's commentary on the words, "And the Virgin's name was Mary." Bernard tells us that no matter what our difficulty, we should look to the star, and call upon Mary: *Respice Stella, Voca Maria*. With her showing us the way we will not get lost. Bernard concludes with the words, "And thus you will know from your own experience that the Virgin's name was Mary"[82] This phrase, "you will know by your own experience," is used by St. Bernard frequently. It is an important phrase in Cistercian spirituality.

We need to stay in touch with our own experiences. That sounds simple enough, but in the spiritual life we can fool ourselves into thinking we are experiencing something just because we have read about it. For instance, we can read a paragraph or two from the sermon quoted above and believe we have had the experience of being devoted to Mary. But Bernard says we must

82. St. Bernard, Second Sermon, *The Glories of Mary*.

have that devotion ourselves, instead of borrowing it from him. To show us how to acquire that devotion, he mentions several types of experiences that leave us feeling lost and alone. For example, he describes the feeling of being adrift in a storm-tossed sea, no longer able to feel solid ground, and says that unless you wish to be swallowed up by it all, look to the star and call upon Mary. "When you are beset with temptations, when you are about to give in to pride, hatred or jealousy, look to the star, call upon Mary. Should anger, avarice or lust violently assail you, look to the star, call upon Mary. If you find yourself beginning to sink into the bottomless gulf of sadness and despair, then think of Mary. Let not her name depart from your lips. Never suffer it to leave your heart. If you do this, you will be safe from deception and will never go astray. You need not fear that you will grow weary and lose heart. You will reach your goal."[83]

What Bernard is describing does not happen overnight. It is a long process. It is the formation of our hearts, and it is rooted in our Cistercian patrimony because since the time of St. Bernard, devotion to Mary has been important to us.

Notice the experiences Bernard describes. We are all familiar with them because they are all part of being human: pride, ambition, hatred, jealousy, avarice, lust, and sadness. We don't like to admit it, but we have experienced all of them many times. What Bernard is telling us is that we don't need to give in to them; we don't have to act on them. Don't hate your brother or cut him down because you are jealous or ambitious. Instead, call upon Mary for strength to endure. If you do this over a long period of time, you will realize that Mary is like a star in your life, a permanent, fixed position of strength. She is a nurturing influence, always there, someone who understands what all of us are going through in our lives.

This is just one little example of how we can express our Cistercian patrimony through the way we live. What I find so appealing is that it is so real. Bernard is talking about genuine human

83. Ibid.

emotions, the negative ones: hatred, anger, lust, or jealousy. We all suffer from them. Instead of offering us a way around them Bernard is giving us a way to use them in a constructive way. We are not told to deny we are experiencing anger or lust or that it is bad to feel this way. But we are told that when we feel we can't handle it anymore, when we feel overwhelmed, we must look outside ourselves, look to the Star, the fixed position of love in our lives. Look to someone who loves us as a Mother. Look to Mary.

This brings me to a point I want to make about the formation of the heart, the formation of a monk. It has to bring us to our knees before it works.

I look back on my years of initial formation as being a very difficult time. Since then there have been a lot of changes, and perhaps formation is easier now. It's true that many of the hard rules have changed. But initial formation is still a difficult period because the dynamic is the same. You are giving up one identity to put on the identity of a monk. When you enter at age nineteen or twenty like I did, your identity has not been fully formed. But if you enter at age forty, it's different because you have a history as a result of having had more life experiences, more accomplishments, and more education. That's why I think initial formation is much more difficult for someone who must dispossess himself of all that history. To give it up in order to take on a new identity as a monk is very difficult.

But no matter when a person enters or no matter how old or young he may be when he begins initial formation, the first five years or so are a time of difficulty and trial. St. Bernard says the first step to becoming a monk is self-knowledge. It is the knowledge that you are weak, you are a sinner filled with a lot of passions, such as ambition and lust and anger, and you can't do much about it except to suffer it to be and ask for God's mercy. The second step is realizing that others are in the same boat, and this leads to compassion. The first step is learning to have compassion for yourself. The second step is learning to have compassion for others.

This is not something that happens simply by reading about it. It is only your own experiences that can teach it to you. As I said, everyone has these experiences. The way we become monks is by applying the principles of the Rule, and the teachings of our Fathers (like Bernard's sermon on Mary) to the particular hardships we are enduring.

There are several key teachings in the Rule that apply only to monks. One is step four of humility. Basically it says to go on with a quiet heart when you feel you have been treated unjustly, being patient amid hardships and even embracing the suffering. We might not always succeed in doing this, but to believe in it as a principle of the monastic life is important.

Another key teaching is found in chapter 5 of the Rule where Benedict says, "They no longer live by their own judgment, giving in to their whims and appetites; rather they walk according to another's decisions and directions, choosing to live in monasteries and to have an abbot over them" (RB 5:12). This doesn't mean you come to the abbot's office every morning and he gives you some kind of direction that goes against your will. It's more like going to the work board and seeing you have been assigned to make caskets even though you thought the novice master had said you could have a retreat day. It's like expecting to be assigned a particular job you were hoping to have, only to discover it was given to somebody else, and you've been left with the short end of the stick.

There are countless times in the course of a day when we are challenged to apply the principles of monastic living to a very human situation. Formation really begins on our knees, when our self-assurance fails us and we realize we cannot do this on our own. It begins when the monastic way seems absurd, the abbot doesn't appear to know what he is doing, and it looks like the rest of the community doesn't care. It's when everything fails us but the crying out for mercy to God and we unite ourselves to Jesus in dark faith. Then we start to be monks.

It's at this point that our pride and our self-sufficiency are gone. There is no such thing as a proud monk. It is a contradiction in terms. I don't think I have ever met a monk who is proud. Monks are humble men, men of mercy and compassion.

We are all engaged in the process of becoming monks. It starts from the first day we enter and ends when we die. It begins just by living the monastic horarium, when we receive the monastic habit and make the first profession. It continues everyday as we pray together, relate to each other in a monastic way, and enter into the monastic culture that is New Melleray.

We have to be careful to preserve this culture. It is our patrimony, a way of living that has almost two thousand years of history and wisdom. We know that some things about our life are not going to change, and this is great. No matter what, we will have Vigils at 3:30 every morning, so we will always be able to count on the early morning hours of silence for prayer and solitude. No matter what we are doing, we will have Lauds and Vespers and the Hours of the Divine Office. The monastic schedule keeps repeating itself day after day, giving us an opportunity to go deeper and deeper into the mystery of Christ's life in us.

In a beautiful essay comparing various types of education Cardinal Newman touches on this aspect of our life. He reminds us that monks are following the path of wisdom, the slow road. What they don't finish in work today they pick up tomorrow because of the beautiful rhythm of the monastic life.

It really takes years to get into that rhythm and to appreciate it. Someone from the outside might see the repetitious consistency of our behavior and think it is boring, but I see men who wouldn't miss the early morning hours of prayer for anything. Short of illness, they will be at Vigils, and perhaps they'll even rise long before Vigils even begins. They have entered a pattern or a rhythm of prayer they wouldn't dream of giving up.

INSPIRATION FROM THE SAINTS

Saints: Gifted with Persevering Faith

While we were awaiting the election of a new pope I was talking to one of the monks at our monastery in Missouri about some of the cardinals who were eligible. He said, "I believe the Cardinal of Paris has a Jewish mother. If he is elected he will be the second Jewish Pope." This caught me off guard and I said, "Who was the first?" He replied, "Peter, of course!" I guess you could say this is "thinking outside the box." I suppose when it comes to the saints we need to think outside the box too. Thinking outside box means expanding our boundaries, opening up our horizons. Take the feast of All Saints, for example—does it mean only canonized saints? Does it mean only Catholic saints? We have the book *All Saints*, by Robert Ellsberg, in our library. It lists saints for each day of the year. It's a very inclusive list that takes into account people like Gandhi, Martin Luther King, Dorothy Day, and Simone Weil, because they are "prophets and witnesses of our time." But even here you have to have been someone quite special to be listed; you have to have achieved some great work that's been recognized as exceptional. When we celebrate the feast of All Saints (November 1), it is even broader than that. On that feast day we commemorate all who have been redeemed by the Blood of Christ. There is "a huge number," the book of Revelation tells us, "impossible to count, of people from every nation, race, tribe and language" (Rev 7:9).

What is a saint? St John tells us a saint is someone who is like God. They are like God because "they see God as he really is" (1 John 3:2). There are saints, and there are saints. The great saints are held up for our admiration and encouragement. They are gifts to the Church, someone like Mother Teresa and Maximilian Kolbe and others like them who have messages for us about how to live. But on the feast of All Saints we also recall the unknown saints—the ones who are now seeing God face-to-face and becoming like him.

If we could examine each of their lives, maybe all we would say about them is that they tried and they believed. They lived as best they could. They persevered in their trust in God. They lived the Beatitudes, perhaps without even knowing it, perhaps without ever knowing they were following the teaching of Jesus. Their desire was true. St Augustine said, when commenting on this passage from St. John's epistle, that the entire life of a Christian is an exercise of holy desire. You do not see what you long for, but the very act of desiring prepares you to receive it.

He goes on to say that by making us wait, God increases our desire. We are in a waiting mode. We have the scent of heaven in our nostrils, but we cannot taste it. We see it in the distance, but we do not possess it. To live this way is not easy. To live in the land of unknowing, or of not understanding, can lead to uncertainty and doubt. But if you look at the lives of the saints, they were anything but uncertain. They were definitely not unsure about what they believed. It is the firmness of their lives that strikes us. They had a firm hold on something they did not understand. Their firmness did not come from their penetrating intellects. It came from their faith. To be a canonized saint you need heroic faith, yet we belong to a family of faith where the heroic acts of one are shared by all.

The saints lived in the land of unknowing just as we do, but their desires were great and their faith gave them a firm hold on the mystery of life. It is our heritage to live without fully understanding. We are not swans, but we paddle along doing the best we can with the gifts we have. "What we shall be in the future has not yet been revealed . . . we shall be like him because we shall see him as he really is." This we can be sure of.

Aspire to Become Saints

"What are you going to be when you grow up?" is a common question adults ask children. Or, if they are old enough to be in high school or college, the question will be, "What are you going to do?" By the time a child is a senior in college, he or she has learned how to deflect the question by having a pat answer, or in rare cases, a real answer, something like, "I am going to law school," or "medical school," or whatever. What you will never hear is, "I am going to be a saint!" If someone said that, we would quickly change the subject and think, "How weird!" You just don't set out to be a saint the way you do to be a lawyer or a doctor. Becoming a saint is something like falling in love. Neither can be carefully planned in advance. You might want to, but you can't make it happen by yourself. Setting out to be a saint on your own is like someone on crutches setting out to run the fastest mile on record; it is just not going to happen.

Becoming a saint is not something you do by yourself. It is something that is done to you. It is like an anointing. It is imposed by another. No one alive has ever said, "I am a saint." If they would, that very statement would have proven they were not!

Suppose five or six people are in a lineup, could you tell which of them was the saint? Never. The way classical artists got around this was by painting a halo around the heads of saints. Without the golden halo they looked like anyone else. Halos are like angels' wings. They are meant to indicate a spiritual quality that cannot be seen. Giotto painted magnificent wings on the archangel Gabriel in his Annunciation painting. But if you ponder the painting and look at the angel, what you see is really a strange creature, a human being with enormous wings! How else is a painter to indicate an angel? Wings don't cut it anymore with modern painters. Van Gogh said he wanted to "paint men and women with that something of the eternal which the halo used to symbolize, and which we seek to convey by the actual radiance and vibration of our coloring."[84] This is a much more subtle approach and perhaps closer to the truth of what we're celebrating on the feast of All Saints.

It's a feast that commemorates even those saints without halos. They may even be people we have lived with, but while they were with us we didn't see the golden glow, even though we always knew they were good people. When the Little Flower died, some of her sisters wondered what in the world they were going to say about her in the circular letter to the other Carmelite convents. She was only twenty-four. What had she really accomplished? Her sanctity was hidden even from those who lived

84. Vincent van Gogh, quoted by Michael Garvey in *Notre Dame Magazine*, Autumn 2004.

with her. It was only years later when we started reading her autobiography, *The Story of a Soul*, that the radiance and vibrating colors of her life caught our eye.

Holiness is like a seed we plant now and harvest later. St. John writes, "My dear friends, we are already God's children, but what we shall be in the future has not yet been revealed" (1 John 3:2). The feast of All Saints is a little peek into the future. It is a little glimmer of hope held out to us to encourage us not to give it all up. We know by faith that we are children of God. What we shall be in the future has not yet been revealed, and it cannot even be imagined. But we know that "we shall be like God because we shall see him as he really is." Right now, St. Bernard reminds us, we only know God in his human face, in his suffering Son. Someday we will know him in his glory. We will know him as we are known by him. Then we too will be saints.

Chapter Five

THE DIVINE OFFICE
AS THE PRAYER OF CHRIST

The Liturgy of the Hours is not just one of the many occupations a monk performs; it is his life. St. Benedict tells him in no uncertain terms that nothing, but nothing, is to be preferred to the "Work of God" (*Opus Dei*, or the Divine Office). What really could be more important than the Work of God? The Divine Office is the prayer of Jesus to the Father, in which we all participate. The words of this prayer are the sacred words of the psalms. Every emotion and thought has an expression in the psalms. They are the cry of all the earth for salvation. The Work of God is the sanctification of the world: "He loved the world so much that he sent his only Son to be our redeemer" (John 3:16). The one praying the psalm is the one sanctified; the ones he prays for in the psalms are the ones sanctified by the Spirit of God. This is the work of salvation continually being acted out, day and night, in the prayer of the Church.

There are seven "hours" of the Office. Each represents a segment of time which is brought into the holiness of God. One "hour" of the Office might last only ten minutes, but taken as a whole, the cycle of prayer several times during the day and night represents the sanctification of every moment of the twenty-four-hour cycle. God is present in everything he creates; he is present in every phase of the universe, in the life cycles of each of us, and even in the daily, weekly, and yearly cycles of time. The Liturgy of the Hours gives us the opportunity to bow to the Presence, to be mindful we live and move and have our being in God. In the liturgy of the Church, we live in a symbolic world; the Fathers viewed the year, which revolves in cycles that never come to an end, as a symbol of eternity. In a real sense, when we enter liturgical time we enter eternity.

You could say that the Divine Office is the human expression of the prayer offered by Jesus to the Father that never ceases. It is the outpouring of love from the Son to the Father, through the Spirit.

Christians in general and monks in particular are exhorted by St. Paul to pray unceasingly. In the pages ahead, I hope to explain this more fully. Briefly stated, it means that at the deepest core of our being, the place called the "heart" in Scripture, we are praying continually, whether we are aware of this or not. Becoming aware is one of the great joys of life. Finding the center, where there is a holy fire of blazing desire rising from our being and joining us to the prayer of Christ, is given only as a gift of grace. If we search for it, we will find it.

To desire it is itself a gift: "The Spirit we have received is not the world's spirit but God's Spirit, helping us to recognize the gifts he has given us. . . . We have the mind of Christ" (1 Cor 2:12, 16). The mind of Christ, the Spirit of Christ, and the prayer of Christ is in us. Our task is to decrease so that he may increase. The paradox is that the more we lose ourselves, the more we find ourselves; the more we give of ourselves, the more we have of ourselves. When we fully decrease to the point of disappearing, we will reappear in Christ, and know ourselves for the first time.

The Liturgy of the Hours

There are several ways to approach a study on the Liturgy of the Hours. The traditional way is to begin with the history of the Divine Office. Another way would be to begin with the concept of prayer. How is the Liturgy of the Hours a nurturing prayer for us? One could also begin with a treatment of the psalms; after all, the psalms make up the greatest portion of the prayer of the hours.

We will indeed touch on all these aspects of the hours, but I would like our entryway into these reflections to be as broad as possible. I would like to situate our study in the context of our whole Christian life, sort of a cultural anthropology.

When we attempt to participate in the Divine Office, or the Work of God, or the Liturgy of the Hours, three synonymous names, we are, to use an analogy, entering into three time zones and one foreign country.

The three time zones are secular time, sacred time, and mythological time. The foreign country is the land of poetry. Poetry is foreign territory for the vast majority of people. Just look at how much shelf space is allotted to poetry in any bookstore.

Let us look at the time zones. Secular time is where we live, where we feel at home. It is the natural air we breathe, our most comfortable environment. One author expresses it like this, "The world in which we live has given birth to us, nurtured us and formed us. We see it, hear it, touch it and suffer its effects every moment of our lives. Our faith on the other hand is abstract, and God we cannot see."[85]

Charles Davis, a British author, adds:

> People are the product of society. . . . The individual comes to be a person only in and through the action of the social environment upon him. From infancy onwards by socialization he internalizes the social reality that surrounds him. That social reality is drawn into his consciousness and is built into him as the structure of his inner life. His thought and imagination, his emotions and activity are ordered into a pattern given by the culture in which he has been formed and he depends upon society for continuance of his attitude and activity, which otherwise would disintegrate and become meaningless. . . . Consider how the language an individual receives from his culture patterns his thoughts and emotions.[86]

85. George Guiver, *The Company of Voices: Daily Prayer and the People of God* (New York: Pueblo Publishing Co., 1988), 3.
86. Op. cit., 4

What I mean by secular time is our dominant culture; there is no way we can survive outside of it. It is inside our skin; it is the way we think and perceive reality.

Now when we come to the liturgy, we enter into another time zone. We are asked to leave aside as much as possible our secular, dominant culture and enter into the culture of the liturgy. The language is different, the movements of our body are different, and the values are different. The liturgy has a different calendar than our civil calendar. The cycles of season and feast days are joined to secular time, but in many ways, the connections are weak. Modern technological culture has obliterated any sense of sacred time. When you consider the amount of hours spent at work, and the chores at home, and various and sundry time-consuming obligations, it is almost ridiculous to talk about the Liturgy of the Hours. Who has time for it? Yet, this is what it is all about, the sanctification of time. If we think of time as a commodity, and it is hard not to, then the sanctification of time makes no sense. But if we think of our life as a sacred journey or as St. Bonaventure says, "a journey of the soul into God," then everything in our life has a potential sacredness about it. Embedded in our secular life is the pearl of great price, just under the surface perhaps, or deep and hidden; either way we must search for it. This is the first movement of a monastic vocation which we all share: the search for God in our life. We cannot confine the liturgy to a given place, the church. When we leave the church we cannot leave God at the door. Developing a sense for the liturgy means applying the insights of the liturgical service in our daily life. This is especially true of the Scriptures used in the liturgy. I love the understanding of our life expressed in de Caussade's *Abandonment to Divine Providence*: "You [God] speak to every individual through what happens to them moment by moment."[87] He goes on to say that the "written word of God is full of mysteries, and equally so is His word expressed in world events. With

---

87. Jean Pierre de Caussade, *Abandonment to Divine Providence* (New York: Doubleday, Image Books, 1975), 43.

our bodily eyes we can see the natural sun and its beams, but the eyes of our soul, by which we want to see God and His works, remain shut."[88]

The eyes of our soul are opened gradually after much struggle, and willpower alone will not bring it about. It is only by believing against all evidence that God is speaking to us through what happens to us moment by moment that we become aware that there is more to our life than what we see; it all depends on the gift of faith. God's care for each of us, his providence, is intimately involved in every detail of our life. One of the meanings of the monastic practice of "guarding your thoughts" is to keep certain thoughts out of your mind. Do not give them entrance. In our context these would be thoughts that undermine our belief that God's providence is guiding our life and that from moment to moment God is with us.

De Caussade presents two types of communication from God. They are the written words of Sacred Scriptures and his Word expressed in world events. He says, "Holy Scripture is the mysterious utterance of a still more mysterious God, and the events of history are the incomprehensible words of this same hidden and unknown God. They are dark drops from an ocean of darkness and shadow."[89]

I like chapter 1 of the Rule of St. Benedict because it tells us that anyone pursuing a life in the Spirit is going to have a struggle, a battle within. An "ocean of darkness" surrounds each of us, but like the flower that pushes through concrete, we know intuitively there is light in that drop of darkness.

One early morning, amidst the dark surroundings, some poetic verses dawned on me:

> Did someone speak to me of love
> this morning?
> Impossible.

88. Op. cit., 42.
89. Ibid., 5.

My morning was as rough as
hack-saw blades cutting through steel.
There was a moment, however,
before dawn
standing by the cemetery
feeling a gentle breeze on my face
hearing the crickets
As I stood with the moon and stars, crickets and trees
The circle seemed to close.
Someone spoke to me of love.

The struggle we have not to let the predominant secular culture completely rule us is not new. It is the basic story of the Sacred Scriptures. It is the story of idolatry—not something we think about very much, but idolatry has many forms. Anything we value more than God becomes a false god. There are in the Hebrew Testament extremely strict laws about not mixing with foreigners—the Ammonites, the Moabites, and the Hittites—anyone that is not a member of the Chosen People. It is not that these nations are evil; it is more that the little group of Hebrews will be assimilated, and Yahweh will be forgotten.

Take the following story found in Isaiah 7. The allies of the Assyrians are besieging Judah; it seems only a matter of time before they overrun all of Israel. The king wants to make an alliance with Egypt to ward off the pending disaster. This seems pretty reasonable to me. But Isaiah goes into cataclysms of anger over this suggestion. He pleads for trust in God, not in military alliance (7:7-11). The psalms are filled with this same theme: do not put your trust in horses or chariots but in the name of the Lord. Iron chariots were the tanks of the time.

When we enter the liturgy, we are entering the culture of God, and from his vantage point we search for the light in the drops of darkness that make up such a large part of our culture. Someone is speaking to us of love, if only we had the ears to hear.

We now move to the third time zone: the mythological zone. In a very real sense we are alienated from this culture, largely because of technology. Our scientific worldview obliterates the world of myth and nature. Myth is an attempt to give us the story of beginnings, the time before historical records. It is the story of Genesis, when God created from the void, what Dylan Thomas calls, "the fields of praise." The "fields of praise" are the fields we stand on in the liturgy. Not only there, but the mystics teach us these fields are everywhere. There is a story in St. Gregory's life of St. Benedict recounting what happened right after the death of the blessed Benedict:

> Two monks saw a magnificent road covered with rich car-peting and glittering with thousands of lights. From his [Benedict's] monastery it stretched eastward in a straight line until it reached up into the heaven. "This is the road," the monks were told, "taken by Benedict when he went to heaven."[90]

We are all walking on such a road, richly carpeted, and glittering with lights, if we only knew it. It is only at the end of our life, when we look back through transformed eyes, that we will realize what the *fields of praise* were really like.

Myths can be understood in many ways. I understand them as nonhistorical stories arising from the deep consciousness of men and women of all cultures. Every civilization has its mythological stories about how their particular race began; ours is in the book of Genesis. Original sin plays such a prominent role in our thinking; we tend to forget the more positive aspects of the story. We are created in the image and likeness of God. This is our essence. The way we experience our essence has been determined by original sin. Instead of walking with God in the garden, the first *fields of praise*, we have been banished and now our most common experience of God is his absence.

At the center of our life is this tremendous experience of emptiness. This gives birth to a passionate longing for fulfillment.

90. St. Gregory the Great, *Life and Miracles of St. Benedict*, chap. 37 (Collegeville, MN: St. John's Abbey Press, 1949).

If we get in touch with this emptiness at a deep level, and do not fill it with trivial substitutions, it becomes a burning desire for God. This in turn gives birth to prayer. Every civilization has tapped into the primordial rhythm of nature that in some mysterious way awakens our desire to pray.

If you want to know the origin of the Liturgy of the Hours you have to look to the depths of the human heart that is touched by the journey of the sun around the earth (cf. Ps 18). The old Catholic axiom that grace builds on nature is nowhere more true than in the Liturgy of the Hours: into the natural rhythm of sunrise and sunset the liturgy inserts the mystery of Christ. The mystery of nature is meant to reveal the mystery of Christ, our Sun of Justice. The two hinges of the day are dawn and dusk— dawn, where darkness gives way to light; dusk, when darkness appears to overcome the light. Both are twilight zones, a mixture of night and day. These are times for silence; change is happening. Our bodies are attuned to this if we are still; our souls thirst for the light about to come forth. Night, of course, reminds us of the sleep of death, but it is a death which evening announces in such a gentle way, a cessation of struggle and ambition, a surrender into the rest of God.

The Liturgy of the Hours is based on the natural rhythms of light and darkness, the journey of the sun across the sky only to descend into the abyss, and from there to rise again, as expressed in the psalms. Psalm 18 (19) is a beautiful manifestation of this worldview:

> The sky proclaims the glory of God;
>   the firmament shows forth
> the work of his hands.
> Day unto day takes up the story;
> Night unto night makes known the message.
> No speech, no word, no voice is heard;
> Yet their span goes forth through all the earth,
> their words to the utmost bounds of the world.
> There he has pitched a tent for the sun—
> It comes forth like a bridegroom coming from his tent,

rejoices like a champion to run its course.
At the end of the sky is the rising of the sun;
to the furthest end of the sky is its course.
There is nothing concealed from its burning heat.

You can see how easy it is to transpose this psalm into the mystery of Christ, the true light of the world, the Sun of Justice. Nothing is concealed from his light. He spans the whole universe with his love. The passage of the sun is a living metaphor for the journey we make each day under the banner of his love. From the rising of the sun to its setting, we praise the name of Jesus.

When Jesus walked the earth, Palestine was part of the Roman Empire. The temple worship, as recorded in the New Testament, uses the Roman method of recording time. Accordingly, there are twelve hours of sunlight and twelve hours of darkness. This is only scientifically true at certain times of the year, but it nonetheless serves as the pattern that the early Church followed and is still used in monasteries to identify the hours of the Divine Office. Sunrise is 6 A.M. This is the first hour of the day, the time of praise, and so the Latin word for praise, "Lauds," is still used as the name for Morning Prayer. Nine A.M. is three hours after sunrise and so it is called "Terce" (Latin for three), midmorning prayer. Twelve noon is the apex of the day, when the sun is directly overhead and is the sixth hour after sunrise, therefore the hour for midday prayer, "Sext" (or six). Nine hours after sunrise is the time for mid-afternoon prayer, "None" in Latin. Terce, Sext, and None are known as the *little hours*, since they are very brief, about fifteen minutes. The setting of the sun is 6 P.M., the time of vespers, meaning "evening praise." The day ends with Compline, or in modern terms "*bedtime* prayers." When dark covers the earth and the sun disappears, time is marked by the four watches of the night. The first watch is from 6 P.M. to 9 P.M. and so on, with three hour intervals until sunrise. The Gospel of Mark mentions the four watches in chapter 13: "Watch, therefore, you do not know when the thief is coming, whether in the evening, or midnight or cockcrow or in the morning." The third watch was called cockcrow. It was from midnight to three in the morning. Jesus told Peter: "In truth, I tell you, this day, this very night, before the cock crows twice, you will have disowned me three times" (Mark 14:30). Finally, there is a reference to the fourth watch of the night earlier in Mark: "And about the fourth watch of the night he came toward them, walking on the sea" (6:48).

If we could diagram the hours of the Divine Office and their relation to the movement of the sun, it would look something like this:

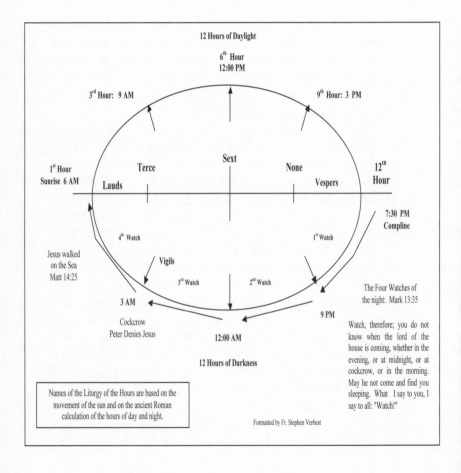

The Desert Fathers would rise at midnight, the hour when the ancients believed the demons were abroad. They would pray that the light of Christ would overcome the darkness of evil. The struggle we are all involved in is played out in the life of a monk keeping vigil for the life of the world.

So far, we have been looking at the hours of the Office in their relationship to the natural cycle of time, following the course of the sun across the sky. This touches something deep in our psyche, but it rests on mythology, and our faith is historical. The call of Abraham marks the beginning of history in the Bible.

We call it salvation history. From this point on we can look for historical markers in the Old Testament. We can validate dates when the great events took place. In Exodus, for example, the journey through the desert is documented by place names. The kings of Israel are recorded, as is the building of the temple. All of these are historical events in which there is a spiritual dimension.

When we come to the New Testament, the mystery of Jesus is presented to us in the context of the Hebrew Testament. Jesus is the new Moses. His sacrifice is the fulfillment of the covenant; he is our Passover. After his death, the sacraments are the continuation of his life on earth. St. Leo says that "our Redeemer's visible presence has passed into the sacraments."[91] The Eucharist is the central mystery of the Church, which is now the Body of Christ on earth; it is the continuation of the Passion, Death, and Resurrection of Christ. The Eucharist, then, is the ultimate prayer, because it is the total self-giving of Jesus to the Father. He gave up his spirit in death, which leads to the total union with God. The self-giving love from the Father to the Son and the Son to the Father in the Spirit is given a human dimension when the Word took flesh. So we can say that the Eucharist is the visible expression of the inner life of the Trinity, but now with all of us participating in this union. Jesus brought us into the inner life of the Blessed Trinity.

91. St. Leo the Great, *Second Sermon for the Ascension.*

Following this line of thought, the Divine Office is the prayer of Jesus to the Father in which we are invited to participate. It is a beautiful blending of mythological time, historical time, and sacred time. Sacred time is eternal time; it is the life of the Trinity shared with us.

On the feast of the Birth of Mary, we have the song of Mary antiphon for Vespers, which is a good example of how the liturgy incorporates nature and history: "O Virgin most prudent, going forth like the bright radiance of the dawn, you are the Daughter of Sion, all beautiful and fair, lovely as the moon, bright as the sun."

The prayer of the Apostolic Church was centered on Jesus. This is what distinguished them from their Jewish community. At first they kept many of the Jewish prayer times of morning and evening. In the Acts of the Apostles, it says that the apostles gathered at the third hour; this was 9 A.M., when the Pentecost event took place (Acts 2:1-15). At noontime, Peter prayed (Acts 10:9); Peter and John were going to the temple area to pray at 3 P.M. So you have Terce, Sext, and None.

Gradually the office reflected or represented the life of Christ in heaven and on earth. The office of Terce represents the coming of the Holy Spirit and the birth of the Church; then Sext and None represent the three hours that Christ spent on the cross.

The second coming of Christ underlines the watching at Vigils, and the rising and setting of the sun. In Matthew's Gospel we read, "For as lightning comes from the east and is seen as far as the west, so will be the coming of the Son of man" (Matt 24:27).

Christians are meant to live in expectation of this coming: the coming of Christ to them personally and to the world at large. We keep Vigil for this very reason.

There are two ways we can approach the mystery of Christ's life and the natural rhythm of time. We can view it as the history of Jesus superimposed on the cycle of the sun, or we can look at Christ as revealing the true meaning of nature.

Take for instance the hymn we often have at Lauds. The hymn is a ninth-century Latin piece, *Lucis Largitor Splendide.* Translated it goes:

O radiant Giver of Light
When dawn serenely follows night
You open wide upon the earth
An untold wealth of priceless light.

You are the world's true morning star
Far fairer than the rising sun
All light you are and day most full
Who warm the dark and narrow heart.
—*Cistercian Office Hymn*

In this hymn, the sun is a symbol, and Christ is the reality. What the sun does in nature, Christ does in our spirit, our life. He lights our way, opens wide our heart, and warms the dark and narrow places of our soul. St. Basil calls the hymns and the psalms we use in the Office "the voice of the Church." No matter how small the community, as they pray the Liturgy of the Hours, they are the voice of the Church.

The Fathers of the Church give us a valuable teaching on how to use the psalms as prayer. St. Athanasius says, "The Psalms seem to me to be like a mirror, in which a person using them can see himself, and the stirring of his own heart; he can recite them against the background of his own emotions."[92] Following this tradition, Cassian tells us how to get to the meaning of the psalms. It is by identifying our thoughts and emotions right in the psalm itself. He says:

We find all our feelings expressed in the psalms, so that by seeing whatever happens [in the Psalms] as in a very clear mirror we understand better and so instructed by our feelings as teachers we lay hold of it as something not merely heard but actually seen, and, as it were, not committed to

92. Taken from the Breviary of the Church, Office of Readings for August 21.

memory, but implanted in the very nature of things; we are affected from the very bottom of the heart, so that we get its meaning not by reading the text but by experience anticipating it.[93]

In another conference, speaking of charity in the psalms, he says:

For if we have experience of the very state of mind in which each Psalm was sung and written we become like the author and anticipate the meaning rather than follow it, i.e., we remember what happened to us and what is happening in daily assaults when the thoughts of them come over us . . . all that subtle forgetfulness has carried off or thoughtlessness has cheated us of.[94]

This is a very monastic way of interpreting the Scriptures in general and the psalms in particular. The Desert Fathers taught that the best way to come to understand the Scriptures is to put them into practice.

There is another principle of interpretation that comes from the Fathers but is really based on a teaching of Jesus after his Resurrection. Speaking to the two disciples on the road to Emmaus, "beginning with Moses and all the prophets, [Jesus] interpreted to them what referred to him in all the scriptures" (Luke 24:27). When these two returned to Jerusalem, they reported what happened to the eleven and those with them. All of a sudden, Jesus stood among them and, after offering them his peace, explained to them that everything written about him in the Law of Moses and in the prophets, and in the psalms must be fulfilled. Thus began the Christological reading of the Hebrew Bible.

Beyond a literal meaning of the words of Scripture, the Fathers developed what is called a spiritual interpretation of the text. Just as there is more to a person than meets the eye, so there is a deeper meaning to the stories in the Bible than the literal meaning can reveal to us. For instance, searching for the mystery

93. Cassian, *Conference*, 14.
94. Ibid., *Conference*, 10:11.

of Christ hidden in the psalms leads to the understanding that the Office is the prayer of Jesus, and as we recite the psalms, we share in the mystery of his prayer to the Father. It is not our prayer so much as the prayer of Jesus. The *General Instruction of the Liturgy of the Hours* says, "generally both the Fathers and the liturgy were correct in hearing in the psalms the voice of Christ calling to His Father, or the Father speaking to His son, as also when they recognized therein the voice of the Church."[95]

This teaching goes back at least to St. Augustine. Commenting on Psalm 85, Augustine says,

> Jesus Christ . . . both prays for us and prays in us and is prayed to by us. He prays for us as our Priest; He prays in us, as our head; He is prayed to by us, as our God. Let us therefore recognize in Him our words, and His words in us. . . . Therefore, we pray to Him, through Him, in Him; and we speak with Him, and He speaks with us; we speak in Him; He speaks in us the prayer of this Psalm.[96]

Reflecting on this and other passages from the Fathers, we can see how the liturgy is a school of prayer. The public liturgy of the Church should be followed by the interior liturgy of the heart. In fact, there is an ancient Syriac text that talks about the one Church of Christ being distributed over three churches, each having its own liturgy: the visible liturgy in the church, the invisible liturgy of the heart, and the celestial liturgy before the throne of God. The invisible liturgy of the heart, like the official liturgy of the Church, is the prayer of Jesus to the Father which is placed in our hearts at baptism; we are given a share in the priesthood of Christ.

I believe it was St. Leo the Great who said, "Christians, become what you are!" In this "becoming" we learn the importance of interior silence. We must be silent so we can hear, so we can

---

95. *General Instruction of the Liturgy of the Hours*, no. 109.
96. St. Augustine's *Sermon on Psalm 85*, quoted by John Brook, in *The School of Prayer* (Collegeville, MN: Liturgical Press, 1992), 55.

listen to the voice of Christ praying in us. We must move from "strenuous to self-acting prayer, from my prayer to the prayer of Christ in me."[97]

The interior liturgy taking place in our deepest heart is the connecting link between the liturgy of the Church and the liturgy of heaven. St. Isaac the Syrian says,

> Make haste to enter into the bridal chamber of your heart. There you will find the bridal chamber of heaven. For these two are one and the same bridal chamber, and it is through one and the same door that you can see into both. The stairway ascending to the Kingdom is actually hidden in the depths of your heart.[98]

Monks are called not only to live the liturgy of the heart but also to be a witness of this reality to the whole people of God. The monastic liturgy should lead one into the heart. For this reason, it has to be simple, even austere. Someone once called the Cistercians the Puritans of the Catholic Church. Our monastic churches are marked by a harmony of simplicity and interiority. There is nothing to excite one's imagination. The purpose for this is to lead one out of the external world into the realm of the invisible, spiritual realm of the praying heart.

The famous liturgist, Anton Baumstark, discerned two distinct currents in the Liturgy of the Hours. One he called the "Cathedral liturgy," the other, "Monastic liturgy." In the Cathedral liturgy, the psalms are chosen to fit the time of day or the particular feast being celebrated. Psalms of praise in the morning and of thanksgiving at Vespers, for example. By contrast, in the primitive Monastic liturgy, monks would recite the one hundred fifty psalms straight through with no regard for particulars of the feast or hours of the day. There are several examples in the lives of the early monks which were meant to convey that a monk

97. Kallistos Ware, *The Power of the Name* (Oxford: Fairacres Press, 1979), 3.

98. Andre Louf, *Teach Us to Pray* (Chicago: Franciscan Herald Press, 1975), 94–95.

at prayer was so taken with the mystery of God that he was out of time; he was timeless. When St. Benedict was living as a hermit in the caves of Subiaco, St. Gregory tells us, he did not even know it was Easter Sunday. There was a similar incident in the life of St. Anthony. After many years of solitude, his acquaintances forced their way into his hiding place and broke down the door. It is said that Anthony "came forth as from some shrine like one who had been initiated in the sacred mysteries and filled with the spirit of God."[99]

This description is filled with liturgical language: *"Coming forth as from a shrine,"* when in fact he was coming out of a cave in the ground, indicates that his external surroundings were indifferent to him. What mattered was his interior soul, which was as one newly baptized filled with the Holy Spirit. Anthony and Benedict achieved the meaning of the liturgy, the prayer of Jesus in them, to such an extent that they were in continual prayer without the need for external rituals. The mystical tradition of the Church teaches an inward journey to *"that which is."* St. Augustine said, "in a flash of a trembling glance he came to, *that which is."*[100]

To arrive at the eternal within the heart, one first has to come to true self-knowledge, that is, know the center of your own soul: your heart. It is there God meets us. In this life we can only experience eternity within us, in a *"flash of trembling glance,"* but in the life to come it will be our whole existence.

Celebrating the Divine Office as Sacrament

The preface for the feast of the Sacred Heart states that the heart of Jesus, from which flowed blood and water, is the fountain of sacramental life in the Church. This means that the love of Jesus symbolized by his heart is the invisible source of grace in the sacra-

---

99. St. Athanasius, *Life of St. Anthony*, chap. 14, The Fathers of the Church, vol. 15 (Washington D.C.: Catholic University of America Press, 1952), 148.

100. St. Augustine, *Confessions*, VII, 17 (New York: The Modern Library, 1949).

ments. In a similar way, our celebration of the Office is a sacrament. The whole community at prayer is the official prayer of the Church. This is a powerful external sign. The source of this prayer is the heart of Jesus because the Office is the prayer of Christ to the Father. We have to be in touch with this, or as St. Benedict states it, "our mind must be in harmony with our voice" (RB 19:7).

The monastic life is a life of prayer, and St. Benedict says nothing is more important than the Work of God, the Divine Office. But the Office has visible and invisible forms. The invisible form is the life of prayer we have outside of the Office: our interior prayer, meditation, mental and contemplative prayer. This is the very heart of our life, and it is up to each of us to develop it.

There is no set time for our interior prayer. Even though it is essential to our life, there are no classes to teach it. Each one is left to himself to make sure his personal prayer life develops. We can encourage each other and help each other. The abbot can teach and preach on prayer, but when you get down to it, it is up to the individual to be faithful to the inner calling of prayer.

I think this is true because prayer is natural to us. St. Basil says no one has to teach us to love our parents or how to breathe. It is the same with prayer: only the inner prompting of the Holy Spirit can help us learn to pray.

Our whole monastic life has this visible-invisible dynamic. Our daily routine has a lot of externals, or observances, and there is really no monastic life without them. But observances are not ends in themselves. They are related to something else. For instance, solitude, silence, renunciation of self-will, and detachment from wealth are all intended to create a space in our life and provide the environment and climate in which we find our true home, our true self: a heart at prayer.

We often speak of the desert as the climate of monastic prayer. Even though we live in community, we still must live with ourselves (*habitare secum*). These words described St. Benedict. He dwelt with himself. This is not easy to do; a monk is bound to dwell in the inner wasteland of his own being. *Alone* is one of the meanings of the word "monk." Paradoxically, it is within this place that we meet the Lord. The journey in the desert is our journey, there to find refreshing springs of water from the rock of our existence (Exod 20:11). This is the mystery of prayer.

Our deserts are much different than those faced by St. Bernard or St. Benedict. We are children of our own age. Our age is characterized by the avoidance of suffering and the denial of death. That is why the psalms are so important for us: they remind us of the fragility of life. "Our years are seventy or eighty for those who are strong and most of these are emptiness and pain." "You have laid me in the depths of the tomb in places that are dark, in the depths." The only way we can live in this type of dread, this experience of emptiness, is by meeting the Lord Jesus in this desert. As a true Hebrew, Jesus lived and prayed the psalms; his identity is hidden in them. Did he find his mission in the psalms as a revelation from the Father? It is worth pondering this question. I think he did because the psalms give us a picture of his life. He is the subject referred to in the psalms; his life was over like a sigh. He was laid in the depths of the tomb; he emptied himself, taking the form of a slave.

Because of Jesus, our very human condition becomes a prayer. We do not need someone to teach us to pray. All we have to do is be authentic in our life and experience who we are. We must simply let ourselves be fully human, and then put on Christ who became fully human for us.

Among monastic communities, there is much talk about the precarious nature of our life because of aging and lack of vocations. We are being called to become aware of the precariousness of our own being through the dread that threatens us. The prospect of closing the monastery seems to be the ultimate dread for a monastic community.

We are called to embrace our precarious situation; human life is marked with finitude. We chant it all the time in the psalms. The response to our weakness is not to flex our muscles, but to beg God for forgiveness, to pass through the anxiety of the moment. It is to cross over with Jesus, to go through death with him to a new life in the Spirit.

Intense Attention at the Liturgy

Chapter 19 of the Rule of St. Benedict is entitled "The Discipline of Psalmody." Composed of only seven short verses, it begins with the premise that the Divine Presence is everywhere, but most especially at the Liturgy of the Hours. Hence, St. Benedict tells us how we should behave in the Divine Presence. Using several scriptural passages to prove his point, he concludes the whole chapter with the words: "let us stand to sing the psalms in such a way that our minds are in harmony with our voices" (RB 19:7). This phrase is a principle of our liturgical prayer. There should be a harmony between our exterior behavior and our interior sentiments. If we are praising God in our words, then we should be doing the same in our hearts.

To strictly harmonize the expressions of the lips with that of the heart is truly difficult. How easily our minds wander off at the Divine Office! We can stand at reverent attention for the Gospel, by stepping out of our choir stalls and facing the altar, and yet if someone asks us what the Gospel was actually about, we can draw a blank. It often happens that the longer you live in the monastery, the more difficult it becomes to keep the harmony between your mind and your voice. Is it not strange that we can say one thing while thinking about something else that is totally unrelated to it? Our minds are very quick. The speed of thought must be faster than the speed of light.

The mass media, especially television, knows this, and consequently all its programming is designed to fit the quickness of the mind. This is very evident during news presentations. Recently I stopped at my sister's house on the way back from a short trip to our Daughter House of Assumption Abbey in Ava, Missouri. Watching the evening news full of information about the war in Iraq was but one item of the broadcast; while the newscaster was speaking, a continuous ribbon of written text was moving along the bottom of the screen to keep viewers informed about what was happening elsewhere. In the left-hand corner was the weather report, while the most current stock market figures were on the right. So there were four things going on at once, and to my surprise I was able to take it all in.

The monastic liturgy seems awfully slow in comparison to what happens in the media. A poor reader or less than lively celebrant is no match for a young and dynamic newscaster, so you can see what the liturgy is up against. Of course, this is not a fair comparison, because monks are not exposed to TV or the hectic pace of life outside the monastery. This is especially evident on Sundays, when the guests who have come for Mass gallop ahead of us during the Creed. Our tempo must appear very slow to them.

But even though we are not subjected to the media, we can still be very distracted during the liturgy. As a matter of fact, we have to make an effort to be recollected all day long. Mindfulness of God is one of the purposes of our monastic way of life. Our Constitutions state clearly: "By constantly cultivating mindfulness of God, the brothers extend the 'Work of God' throughout the whole day." This is an interesting statement because it suggests that we are to prolong the Office, the Work of God (*Opus Dei*), or the prayer of the Church, throughout the day. We are to do it by staying focused on God, by living *in aspectu divinitatis* (in the sight of God).

Let us consider the Holy Week liturgy. In it we are celebrating some of the most intense events in the life of Christ, and the ceremonies of Holy Week are meant to lead us into the very drama of Christ's final week on earth. We reenact his last days; we take part in his entry into Jerusalem. We are present at the Last Supper; we stand at the foot of the cross. We are baptized into his Resurrection and go with the women to the tomb. All of these we do liturgically, and it can be very difficult for us to keep our minds and voices together. The many rubrics can be more distracting than helpful if we are not careful. Given the complexity and abundance of liturgical ceremonies, it is understandable that we can easily be distracted from what these ceremonies intend to convey and evoke.

One useful practice is to try entering into the attitude of the people who were involved in the historical event we are enacting: the people waving the palm branches, the disciples at the Last Supper, the women at the tomb. Our liturgical texts and songs actually put their words into our mouths. We should, then, according to St. Benedict's principle, have their sentiments in our hearts. Before the liturgy begins, it is helpful to look over the texts to be used and try entering into their meaning by making them our own.

During Holy Week, there are some wonderful patristic texts read at Vigils and Lauds. These are often mystagogical homilies, that is, homilies based on the mystical interpretation of the Scriptures but applied to the liturgical ceremonies. For example, at Vigils of Palm Sunday, we read a passage from St. Andrew of Crete which says, "So let us spread before His feet not garments or soulless olive branches, which delight the eyes for a few hours, and then wither, but ourselves clothed in his graces or rather clothed completely in Him!" (Liturgy of the Hours, Office of Readings, Palm Sunday). St Andrew goes on to say that since we have put on Christ in baptism, we are the rewards of his victory. This is what we should present to him then. The palm branches represent the joy of his victory over sin and our incorporation into his saving action. As St Andrew says, "Let our souls take the place of the welcoming branches as we join today in the children's song."

We are the rewards of his victory. We offer to Christ our very selves. If we can make the offering of ourselves the center of our Palm Sunday celebration, then we will enter fully into the ceremony. It helps to take a period of silence before the liturgy begins to make a prayer of self-offering.

Who is the self that is the reward of Christ's death? It is our whole self, not just the self we are when alone in prayer or at the liturgy, but the total self. It is our life with all its relationships, efforts, and workings. It is not just the mental self, but the body-spirit self, the complexity of our life. It is everything that goes up to make our day. It is also our whole past life as well as our future self. It is whatever will happen to us and whatever we will do. "Let us," St. Andrew says, "present the conqueror of death, not with mere branches of palms but with the real rewards of His victory. Let our souls take the place of the welcoming branches."

This is truly a joyous procession; we are the rewards of Christ's victory. We offer ourselves to him, and sing songs of praise, adoration, and thanksgiving because he shares his victory with us. But as soon as the procession is over and we hear the reading from Isaiah, the mood changes, and we enter into the sorrow of the Passion. Truly our minds are quick. We can change rapidly.

In his second sermon for Palm Sunday, St. Bernard says it was the same people in the same place at the same time, with only a few days in between, who welcomed him with triumph, and afterwards nailed him to the cross. How different, says St. Bernard, are the cries, "Blessed is He who comes in the name of the Lord, Hosanna in the highest," from what the crowd cries later on when they shout, "Away with Him, away with Him, crucify Him!"

To our shame, we recognize our place in that crowd shouting blessings one day and curses the next, and so compunction is part of our Holy Week celebration. It is the compunction we feel for our sins and the sins of the world. It is part of every liturgical celebration.

Conclusion

NIGHT AND THE MONK

It is 3:15 A.M. I just got out of bed and am making my way to the church for night vigils. I was once asked, why do you get up so early? I answered, because we are lax! The ancient monks arose at midnight. Midnight was the chosen hour because it represents the nadir of darkness, the most bewitching hour of the night, symbolic of sinister activity and evil. Demons were thought to roam about at that hour. Watching and praying through the night was a spiritual combat with the forces of evil. This symbolism is lost on our modern society, disconnected from nature as it is. This is not to say the forces of evil have vanished too. Monks keep alive the connection of light and darkness and what they stand for in the deep recesses of the human heart. Rising in the night to pray is a call, a vocation. Pray the new day into being, pray that goodness will overcome evil. Some people suffer from night terrors or restlessness during the night and have told us it is a consolation to them to know that, as they toss and turn, the monks are just getting up to pray. It helps them get through the night.

I make my way to the church by way of the cemetery walk. The moon is floating just above the horizon to the southeast, a pale warm light in a lace of clouds. I stop for a moment to take in the scene, the beauty, the stillness. I look up at a patch of sky suffused in mellow light, subdued and quiet, clouds feeding the moon. Everything is still: the birds are still, the frogs in their pond down the hill are still. Everything is at attention, on review as the parade of clouds passes before the moon. I too stand at attention, and offer my presence. A profound silence envelops me, but the tower bell strikes, and I continue on my way to vigils, the night watch. In ancient times, walled cities had a watchman on the ramparts during the night to warn of danger. In America, we have no walled cities, but we still need someone to watch over the soul of our nation, someone to cry out to God for justice in our world.

As I enter the church, the silence of the night comes with me as if it entered my heart through the still night air. I did not expect it; it came as a gift, a helping presence, a friend at my side. The beauty of the night, the soft glow of the moon, the utter stillness of nature at this hour before dawn is now in my heart. It is one with me. Did I enter the silence or did it enter me? Was I drawn out of myself, or was I deep within myself? I did not know or care to know.

As Vigils began with the familiar words, "O Lord, open my lips and my mouth will proclaim your praise," I entered a stream of prayer as old as the rivers of the earth. I put on a thousand-year-old soul and drank from the wells of wisdom contained in the psalms. Ancient words became my own, expressing sentiments of love and praise and blessing, words of pain and anguish and longing—above all, longing. Longing rises in my heart with the intensity of "a dry weary land without water" (Ps 63). During times of drought, which the monastery farm occasionally experiences, I can almost feel the earth pleading for rain. I long with it and feel the exhilaration when rain finally comes and life springs up from the soil. So it is with the soul longing for God.

Longing is born of absence, praise of fullness. We walk through life on these two legs, absence and presence, consolation and desolation. To run from one is to diminish ourselves. The original meaning of "religion" is to bind together. Our modern world is so fragmented and disconnected. Some say the meta-story, the story that gives us meaning and helps us find our identity, no longer exists. Maybe for some this is true, but for the monk, for the Christian, the story of salvation history is a true history, and it is more than that: it is a metaphor for our personal life. It tells us how to find ourselves.

To find our soul we need the experience of absence as well as presence. We need the nourishment of the still night and the glorious sun, the borrowed words of ancient prayers, the companionship of friends, and above all true love. All these come to us from beyond and form our heart where a matching beauty is brought to life by the gentle touches from soul to soul: "Deep is calling on deep in the roar of mighty waters" (Ps 42).

As the chanting continues, verses of the psalms float by me like stars in the night sky, illuminating and revealing who I am and my place and purpose in the world. All the emotions of the heart are validated by these cries from the heart of our earth. Not only validated, but also consecrated, made holy, and brought into the mysterious providence of God. The psalms give soul to our emotions. Sentimentality is feeling without soul. The modern pace of life leaves little time for soul work. The morning is for rushing, and the night for sleeping; we are disconnected from the natural rhythms of the times and seasons of the year.

This inability to commune with nature is made worse by the demands technology puts on us, but technology is not the cause of it. Every generation since the Fall has had the painful experience of isolation and alienation from life around us. The holy ones tell us the road to presence is through absence. We cannot begin to understand until we suffer it to be. Poets talk about loving the dark hours of their being. To embrace our total self means to accept all our limitations and contingencies. We can, after all, die at any moment. We cannot function very well if that thought paralyzes us, but we cannot ignore it either. To cherish the light, we have to pass through the dark.

One of the Desert Fathers said there is nothing weaker than a monk. This I firmly believe to be true; a monk makes himself vulnerable to the fragility of life. He goes defenseless into the desert where there is no place to hide, where there is nothing to help him forget the great and vast emptiness within. How we run from this emptiness, but we can never evade it for long. Life sets a table of sorrow, and we all must partake of it at one time or another. Saints seem to be the ones who understand this best. To love and to suffer is a phrase they often use.

Perhaps the most poignant reminder of this is the death of a loved one, the ultimate absence. It seems to me that just under the surface of everyone's life, there is this pain of absence. If we ignore it, we cut off half our existence, and before long, we do not know who we are. Few are the ones who are willing to grieve their own existence. To grieve "not who you are but that you are."[101]

Vigils ended and I went back out into the cool summer night. The clouds had disappeared, and just as the moon brought softness to the harsh night, the stars brought a brilliance that took my breath away. Orion was huge in the east, and just above my head were the Gemini twins, Castor and Pollex. They reminded me that we move toward our goal together. Absence and presence do not stand alone; they are twins coming from the same source. The source is not some distant star or impersonal fate. The stars can dazzle us and cheer us on, but they cannot determine our life. The practice of religion, not the study of religion or thinking about religion, discloses and discerns a divine presence and purpose for each of us, a divine vocation. It is a personal God who is involved in the very fabric and texture of our being.

I believe it was Helen Keller who said it is terrible to be born blind, but it is worse to have eyes and not see. The nighttimes of our life, the wintry seasons, teach us how to see and to look deeply into things and take the measure of our being. We are not ruled by fate, or luck, or destiny. There is a purpose behind everything we do and endure, not only an immediate purpose that we can name and explain, but also an ultimate purpose that can only be summed up at the end of our life. There is one who "discerns my purpose from afar, who knows my resting and my rising" (Ps 140). This same holy poem tells us, "Every one of your days was decreed before one of them came into being." If this is so, where is our freedom? It is in our choices. We are free to choose what kind of person we want to be. We move into the future making choices guided by our conscience, discerning the path of truth. As we journey on, we pray, "O search me, God, and know my

---

101. *Cloud of Unknowing*, chap. 44 (New York: Pendle Hill by Harper, 1948).

heart. O test me and know my thoughts. See that I follow not the wrong path and lead me in the path of life eternal" (Ps 139).

I began a silent meditation by entering the solitude of my own being. This is a journey in itself. First, I bring my body into tranquil attention, breathing slowly in and out. Then the inner struggle begins. It seems that when your body becomes quiet and even weightless, a curtain goes up, and your emotional life comes at you like the furies. Thoughts and feelings float to the surface of your mind and demand to be resolved. I let them pass and try to guard my heart against their intrusion. Not to repress them, but just let them pass on. I know they will visit me later in the day. I can deal with them then. Now is the time to move beyond them into a deeper part of my soul. In stages, I visit all my faculties, just to greet them, and ask them to be silent for a little while. I silence my memory, my imagination, even my intellect and will. Finally, I come to an awareness of my naked being, stripped of all my faculties except my very presence before God. Here I give myself away and disappear into God. This is a place, and yet, it is no place. Willpower alone will not bring us here. It is a gift just as the beauty of the night is a gift. Tradition calls this place the heart. It is in everyone; it is the place where God's life flows into our life. It is a meeting of our spirit with God's spirit, where two become one in the transformation of love.

The great silence was ending, and as the sun was rising, the monks were coming together again to pray to the Sun of Justice to bring peace to the world this very day. As the rays of the sun stretched further and further into the long day ahead, I thanked God for "the wonders of my being, for the wonders of all creation" (Ps 139).